THE ESSENCE OF RELIGION

Sayyid Muḥammad Bāqir al-Sīstānī

Translated by
Salim Salhab

Originally published in 2017 in Arabic
This English edition is first published in 2025

Author: Sayyid Muḥammad Bāqir al-Sīstānī
Translator: Salim Salhab

ISBN: 978-1-7384949-6-5

© AIM Foundation 2025

All rights reserved. No part of this publication may be reproduced, stored in a retrieval system, or transmitted in any form or by any means, digital, electronic, mechanical, photocopying, recording, or otherwise, or conveyed via the internet or a website without prior written permission of the publisher, except in the case of brief quotations embodied in critical articles and reviews.

بِسْمِ اللَّهِ الرَّحْمَنِ الرَّحِيمِ

*In the name of God, the Merciful,
the Compassionate*

Contents

Foreword 11
Translator's Preface 15
    Purpose of Translation 15
    Semantic Fidelity over Literal Accuracy 16
    Translation Challenges and Methods 17
Author's Preface 23
Introduction 29
    Importance of the Investigation 29
    Tools of the Investigation: 30
    Necessity of certainty in Religion 34
    Quranic Logic on Conviction 35
    Research Methodology and Overview 39

The Essence of Religion

Religion as a Defined Perspective 47
    Two Alternative Worldviews 48
    Impact of Diverging Worldviews 50
        Dimensions of Religious Worldview 51
Religious Epistemology 55
    Value of Human Cognition 55

   Forms of Epistemological Support 56
   Respect for Human Reason 59
   Two Pillars: Intellection and Devotion 60
   Divine Assistance for Creation 62

Religious Cosmology 67
   Truths of the Creator 68
      Existence of the Creator 68
      Creator's Attributes: Life, Power, Knowledge 68
      Creator's Wisdom 70
      Purpose of Creation 71
      Creator as a Non-Material Being 73
      Unity of the Creator 74
      Limits of Human Comprehension 75
   Creator as the Universe's Regulator 76
      Sustaining the Universe 76
      Divine Authority Over Creation 77
      Gradual Creation of the Universe 78

Religious Anthropology 83
   Divine Care for Humanity 83
      Humanity as the Creator's Steward 84
      Universe Prepared for Humanity 85
      Divine Care from Inception 86
      Allah's Grace (*Lutf*) Toward Humanity 86
      Creator's Love and Affection 89
      Granting Serenity to Humanity 91
      Life as a Test for Humanity 92
      Creator's Message to Humanity 94
      Commitment to Guardianship (*Wilāya*) 94
      Two Divine Systems: Existential (*Takwīnī*) and Legislative (*Tashrīʿī*) 96
      Compensation for Human Suffering 100

- Error of Prescribing Things to Allah 103
- Human Nature and Destiny 104
  - Innate Awareness of the Divine 104
  - Life Beyond Death 107
  - Divine Guidance for Humanity 108
  - Ethical and Mechanistic Laws 111
  - Creator's Non-Neglect of Humanity 113
- Religious Legislation 117
  - Alignment of Law with Human Nature 117
  - Innate Basis of Religious Law 118
  - Depth of Religious and Human Laws 118
  - Religious Law and Innate Rights 120
  - Legislation and Noble Traits 124
  - Legal Rulings and *al-Maʿrūf* and *al-Munkar* *126*
  - Clear vs. Ambiguous Rights in Sharīʿa 127
  - Wisdom in Ambiguous Areas 128
  - Two Pillars of Religious Law 135
  - Example of Religious Education 135
  - Key Matters in Religious Law 139
    - Understanding Human Emotions 139
    - Noble and Habitual Emotions 139
    - Ordinary Desires and Noble Feelings 142
    - Causes of the Second Category of Emotional 144
    - Misattributing Nobility to Ordinary Emotions 149
    - Innate Human Disposition: Simple Yet Complex 151
    - Religious Law and Innate Principles 152
    - Examples of Ambiguous Legislation: 153
    - Clarifying Ambiguous Legislation 153
    - Identifying the Problem in Legislative Matters 154
    - Division of Islamic Legislation 155

Considering Religious Values in Judgment 167
Caution in Opposing Assumed Legislation 175
Absolute and Limited Establishment of Rulings........................... 189
Enforceable and Unenforceable Rulings 195
Classification of Variable or Unenforceable Rulings................... 197

Foreword

It is with great honour and profound gratitude that I introduce *The Essence of Religion*, a work that offers a deeply insightful exploration of the core principles of our faith. This text, written by His Eminence Sayyid Muḥammad Bāqir al-Sīstānī—son of one of the most influential Shia religious authorities of our time, Grand Ayatollah Sayyid ʿAlī al-Sīstānī—provides us with a precious resource for reflecting on the spiritual and intellectual foundations of Islam.

In today's world, where religion is often questioned and misunderstood, *The Essence of Religion* serves as a beacon, guiding us to rediscover the profound and universal principles that underpin our faith. Through this book, we are encouraged to reflect deeply on the relationship between humanity and the Divine, and on how we can apply the wisdom of our tradition to our daily lives.

I would like to take this opportunity to express my deep appreciation for the author, Sayyid Muḥammad Bāqir al-

Sīstānī, whose contribution to Islamic thought is both profound and far-reaching. As the son of the revered Grand Ayatollah Sayyid Ali al-Sistani, he carries forward a legacy of scholarship, leadership, and unwavering dedication to the truth. His ability to convey complex theological concepts with clarity and depth speaks to his remarkable intellect and spiritual insight. This book is a testament to his commitment to enriching the lives of those who seek knowledge and guidance.

I am also immensely grateful to Salim Salhab, the translator, whose careful and thoughtful translation has made this important work accessible to English-speaking readers. The task of translating such a nuanced and intricate text is no small feat, and Salhab has done so with great attention to detail, ensuring that the meaning of the original Arabic is faithfully conveyed while making the text understandable and engaging for a broader audience.

I would also like to extend my heartfelt thanks to the AIM publications team, whose dedication and hard work have been instrumental in bringing this project to fruition. Their collective efforts reflect the values of collaboration, service, and devotion that are at the heart of AIM's mission. A special word of gratitude is due to the generous donors whose support has made this publication possible. Their contributions, both financial and moral, reflect their belief in the importance of knowledge and education. By supporting this project, they have ensured that this valuable work reaches not only those who will read it today, but also future generations.

May Allah accept this effort, guide us to the truth, and grant us the strength to live by the values He has revealed.

Wa Min Allah Al-Tawfiq.

Sayyid Sāmir Al-Ḥaidarī
Chairman, Ahlulbayt Islamic Mission (AIM)

13th Rajab 1446 AH
14th January 2025

Translator's Preface

In presenting this translation of "The Essence of Religion" by al-Sayyid Muḥammad Bāqir al-Sīstānī, I feel both honoured and deeply responsible for introducing this work to an English-speaking audience. This project has been the most ambitious one I have undertaken, requiring a delicate balance between faithfulness to the original text and clarity for readers unfamiliar with the Arabic language and its cultural nuances. This preface serves to explain the purpose of this translation, the challenges encountered, and the strategies employed to convey the essence of this book.

Purpose of Translation

The translation of this work arose from the pressing need for a comprehensive resource in the West that explores the epistemic foundations of religion while addressing its multifaceted dimensions with depth and nuance. In an era characterised by a wide spectrum of opinions on religion—

ranging from fervent advocacy to vehement critique—this book serves as a unique and powerful primer. It encourages readers to engage with the foundational aspects of religion, particularly its relationship to human cognition, morality, and their ultimate purpose. Furthermore, it seeks to rekindle an understanding of the dynamic and reciprocal relationship between human beings and God.

Another goal of this translation was to bridge the gap between scholarship and the youth, making al-Sayyid Muḥammad Bāqir al-Sīstānī's insights available to both academic audiences and reflective general readers. By translating this work into English, there is the hope to foster a deeper appreciation and understanding of religion, particularly Islam and its relevance to each and every person.

Semantic Fidelity over Literal Accuracy

One of the key decisions in this translation was to adopt a less literal, more semantic-based approach. This choice was made after a degree of consideration, recognising the significant differences between Arabic and English in their linguistic structures and stylistic conventions. Arabic prose often employs intricate sentence structures, rich intertextual references, and a cadence deeply rooted in its cultural and linguistic milieu. Translating these elements word-for-word into English frequently results in awkward, convoluted, or overly rigid sentences.

Instead, I prioritised clarity and accessibility, striving to retain the original meaning and essence of the text. This often involved rephrasing certain passages, restructuring sentences, and rarely, reordering the sequence of ideas to align with English norms. If one decides to compare between the two, one will frequently find, for example, the use of a technique called *hysteron-proteron*—which is the reversing of the order of words or clauses. Arabic often presents ideas in a sequence prioritising emphasis or rhythm. In fact, most of the time, it is simply forced to do so because of the nature of the grammar, which, when translated literally, can appear unnatural in English. Reversing this order ensures coherence and readability for English-speaking audiences.

Additionally, Arabic prose tends to allow sentences to flow continuously without punctuation for extended lengths, relying on conjunctions and context for coherence. In English, shorter sentences are generally more effective in maintaining the reader's attention and ensuring understanding. As such, this translation frequently divides long Arabic sentences into smaller units, preserving their interconnectedness while improving readability.

Translation Challenges and Methods

The translation of Quranic verses presented a unique challenge. These verses are central to the author's arguments and carry layers of meaning that require careful handling. To ensure both accuracy and resonance, I drew on established translations by M.A.S. Abdel Haleem, Dr. Mustafa Khattab, and Sahih International. Each of these translators offers a distinct angle and style, and their works served as invaluable references. However, I did not adopt these translations verbatim. Instead, I edited and adapted them to suit the context in which the verses appear in the text, ensuring they complemented the narrative and the arguments advanced by al-Sayyid al-Sīstānī, whilst also trying to remain as faithful as possible to the original Arabic of the verses.

Some of the concepts or jargon discussed in "The Essence of Religion" are deeply rooted in the Islamic context of the writer, and can be challenging to convey in English. Terms such as "*fiṭra*", for example, carry charged connotations in Arabic that lack precise equivalents in English. In such cases, I opted for a rough translation combined with a transliteration of the term, since it is assumed that the vast majority, if not entirety of the audience are Muslims. I hope that this will allow readers to understand these terms without overcomplication or distortion.

I tried to avoid overly ornate language that might alienate contemporary readers while attempting to maintain the dignity and gravitas of the original work. The aim was to produce a translation that resonates with both specialists and general readers.

At its heart, "The Essence of Religion" is a wholehearted meditation on the human condition and its relationship with the Divine. The author invites readers to reflect on the foundational questions of existence: What is the purpose of life? How do human beings understand and engage with God? How does God engage with humans? How do the various dimensions of religion—ritual, ethics, and theology—coalesce to form a coherent worldview? These questions are as relevant today as they were centuries ago, transcending any social, political, or cultural boundaries.

In a world increasingly marked by division and misunderstanding, this book offers a counter-narrative rooted in nuance, depth, and intellectual rigour. It challenges simplistic dichotomies between faith and reason, tradition and modernity, and the individual and the collective. By exploring the epistemic foundations of religion, it equips readers with tools for engaging with religious thought critically yet respectfully.

This translation would not have been possible without the support and contributions of many individuals. I am deeply indebted to the works of previous translators and scholars whose efforts in making Islamic texts accessible to English-speaking audiences paved the way for this project. I would like to express a specific thanks to Alaa al-Muradi, who recommended the book be translated and helped in setting up this project. Otherwise the list of those to thank would span for quite long...

Lastly, I pray for the health and divine success of al-Sayyid Muḥammad Bāqir al-Sīstānī, who despite his relatively young age as a scholar, has written many works of great depth that address the up-and-coming generation. His work can be described as a contribution that addresses the timeless questions of humanity in a fairly straightforward manner.

May this book illuminate the minds and hearts of its readers, sparking reflection and dialogue on the questions it raises and the answers it provides.

Salim Salhab

7th Rajab 1446 AH
8th January 2025

Translator's Preface

Author's Preface

All praise be to the Lord of the Worlds and may peace and blessings be upon all of the Prophets and Messengers, especially Muḥammad and his immaculate and pure progeny.

This work investigates and explores a number of questions regarding how one can religiously ground themselves, which aim to seriously help the person searching for religion during their greater journey of finding the Truth, so that they may enlighten themselves by it. This is because one does not find a journey of higher-stakes in the life of a person. For the life of a human is either a fleeting moment in the history of the universe which will cease at their death, or it is an eternal one that is continued after death in another realm. Likewise, the deeds of humans are either meaningless time-bound actions, or they have everlasting effects in terms of happiness and misfortune.

This life is either a pasture where the human lives for mere moments, or a racetrack in which people compete and race for cognisance and virtue; so that each one of them may seize the pay-off for their deeds tomorrow. Thus, it is required for any searcher to concern themselves with this matter appropriately, due to its grand scale and importance.

These investigations were not—in terms of their general origins and premises—founded in an attempt to defend religion, nor to convince people of it, nor for the sake of arguing in favour of a previously assumed position; in fact, they are the consequence of contemplation about the reality of this life and the different viewpoints concerning it, and the gravity of the religious perspective on this subject. This was after having tirelessly revised the established religious texts, continual and sustained reflection about the bases of this viewpoint, its tenor, direction and foundations, in addition to having to interpret the *prima-facies* and ambiguous texts within it, in the hope of reaching at a conception of religion that the writer himself can grasp and enlighten himself through in life, taking it as the utmost goal in his everyday behaviours and deeds. This is since the matter of religion is not one that a rational person can ever consider to be a means of ensuring some sort of personal or societal gain, nor a tribal matter where a person ascribes themselves to the beliefs of their people or predecessors, nor is it a research that is conducted as a pastime, sitting as a mere footnote in the encyclopaedia of life. Rather, the matter of religion is one that is worthy of being in the very epicentre and forefront of human concerns in life, where one remains advising oneself, being truthful in their choices, serious when reflecting, living the search and the stages that accompany it, until they come to a solid conclusion that their intellect can attest to, to which a person can feel tranquility, whose correctness can be guaranteed by intuition, and one which a person can take responsibility for, in terms of all the effects that extend from it by consequence.

I have strived hard so that my research regarding religion addresses all matters related, starting by understanding religion for what it claims to be, portraying it for what it truly is, without imposing values on it that it does not acknowledge, and without engaging in contrived interpretations of the religious texts that do not accord with available information, relying primarily on the Glorious Quran, which paints the foundations of the religious path on the authority of Allah (may He be Glorified) in a clear-cut manner, followed by the luminous Prophetic traditions, and the words of Imam 'Alī (peace be upon him) in *Nahj al-Balāgha*, which in reality can be said to be an explication of the Holy Quran and a presentation of its messages in yet another eloquent manner.

It is also important to note that this book—aside from clarifying the foundational and definite matters from the religion—comprises the mention of possible theories that pertain to its branches and extensions, which we do not intend for people to necessarily uphold, neither are they representative of a specific jurist's opinion from amongst the jurists of the Muslims. Instead, the context required defining the limits of what the religious perspective can cover when examined objectively. Perhaps, as a consequence of this condition, the most broad interpretation of religion was presented.

As a consequence, some of the mentioned perspectives may be a position held by some scholars in light of their *ijtihād* (independent legal reasoning), or a valid view in interpreting some of the religious texts, and the discussion as to how decisive or reliable these texts are, is left to the research of specialists. Likewise, the level of presentation in most places in this work—despite what is mentioned within in terms of verses and narrations—does not qualify as a book of detailed technical substantiation, and thus what can be easily understood is primary in this text.

This, along with the branching nature of the book's subject matter, has made it necessary to express points concisely. In fact, it has led us to select a number of relevant topics from among the many that could have been discussed, although I have tackled some of them in more detail in the book: *Tazkiyat al-Nafs wa-Taw'iyatiha* (Purifying the Self and Rendering it Aware).

These investigations were originally a number of talks that were given with a group of scholars at a limited opportunity, with additions that were necessary due the tangents and demands dictated by the subject. The intended audience of the discourse, in particular, were esteemed young people studying in universities, institutes, and various centres of learning and education, to assist them in serious contemplation regarding the reality of this life and its objectives.

A number of dear people took great care in preparing these lectures, who were all present, and they have exerted much effort, which is greatly appreciated... while it is the case that they continue to require further examination, reflection and investigation, yet, they remain suitable as an initial attempt. My success is only from Allah, upon Him I rely and to Him I delegate my affairs.

Introduction

We have come to know that this study, in its entirety, is an accessible introduction for a person's substantiation of the matter of religion and its trueness, so that this substantiation may be based on clear equations and definite principles, which will protect them from falling into theoretical and practical doubts and errors.

It is incumbent before diving into the proceeding investigations, to provide an introduction that comprises several matters:

Importance of the Investigation

The First Matter: Is that the importance of this investigation lies in its impact on the life of a human.

This is because religion—in reality—is nothing but a cosmological worldview that explains the dimensions of this life, proceeding to establish three greater truths, which are: The existence of Allah (Glorified and Exalted is He), His message to the human being, and the permanence of the human after this life, either in a state of happiness or misfortune, in accordance to their actions and behaviours throughout it.

It is imperative that these realities are understood by every human and that they take a position on these issues; for researching them is not an intellectual hobby that is conducted for the sake of quenching one's thirst for perusal, such as researching the cosmos and its galaxies. Neither is it done in pursuit of happiness, nor is it a means to ensure comfort and so forth; rather, researching these realities is a search into the very core of human life; because it specifies the fundamental values that underpin one's practical activities, considering the fact it provides a clear approach in the case that one affirms or accepts the probability of these truths... This, as opposed to a situation where a person definitively negates such matters, for then, they would be freed from their dictates and safeguarded by the dangers of opposing them.

Tools of the Investigation:

The Second Matter: Is that the tools of the investigation are the self-evident matters that the rational faculty can cognise, both theoretical and practical.

This investigation relies on tools which are clearly cognised by the rational faculty, that can be said to be from the self-evident matters of general human life, which are deeply ingrained with every step we take, and in every particular from amongst its particularities; this is because it is well-known that human life depends on two types of cognition...

One is: Cognising things using the rational faculty; we all concede our existence, our senses, limbs, matters that are clear in front of us, in terms of individuals, tools, foods and the like. We also engage with these things, proceeding in all of these matters on the self-evident basis of the value of human cognition, whilst also engaging in the process of verification in matters that are subject to error.

If a person claims that there is no value to human cognition then they are in reality, asserting that they themselves are incorrect; because every action and reaction of this claimant is premised and dependent on this very cognition, whether they are aware or unaware of it.

And the other is: To cognise the principles of behaviour and actions in life. This part is the basis of laws that organise both the individual and communal life of the human being. In reality, it is the cornerstone of all laws that states and governments rule by. This is the case even if they may disagree on some details of this law due to the fact that not everyone possesses the same precision when it comes to cognition, or in terms of the tools that safeguard the law, or due to impulses that win a person over and the like.

It is not possible for a human to reject the existence of laws that govern human life that can be cognised by the rational faculty, in addition to determining that they are to be enforced and abided by so that his life can remain secure, how could it be otherwise?! For I have found the canons, societal etiquettes, in all their various forms; whether conventional (*'urfiyya*), statutory (*waḍ'iyya*), or Islamic (*shar'iyya*), in addition to family, tribal and governmental laws that have been produced for this very goal.

And since this study proceeds from these self-evident axioms and derives the value of its conclusions on the basis of their value, it is thus an intellectual obligation for every rational person who acknowledges them.

And perhaps some of those who delve into philosophy have doubted the value of human cognition and trust in it, while others have denied it altogether. However, refuting such doubt or denial does not require more than drawing the attention of the doubter or denier to the fact that they themselves rely on cognition in every action they undertake, even in their denial of the value of cognition entirely. For this very denial is itself an act of cognition and an intellectual judgement, and it is also based on a set of cognitions. This is because they aim to communicate the value of this cognition to others, which involves affirming the existence of others and their ability to comprehend what they are saying, and seeking to persuade them using tools appropriate to their thinking and understanding. All of this is nothing but engagement with realities that are cognised.

In the same way that some of those who have delved into ethics and its epistemic value, or have found that there are no ethical principles to life, but rather the human being proceeds in their emotions and actions from a point of strength or weakness.

Except that this doubt and rejection is one which is merely theoretical and is contradictory—in practice—with what every human life is premised on in terms of its dealings with others. Thus, responding to this does not require more than alerting the doubter and rejecter to the fact that they themselves proceed to engage with their families, children, friends, parents, neighbours, teachers, and bosses with decency and proper manners, whilst also expecting the same in kind. If they were treated with disrespect by their son, hen they would reprimand him for behaving like this with his parent. Likewise if a person reneged on a prior agreement with them, they would proceed to reprimand them for reneging the agreement... All of these reprimands are premised on the idea of ethical conceptions.

Thus, it has become clear based on the above: That the origin of the epistemic value of human cognition—in the two aforementioned forms—are the primary principle for human life, from which one proceeds in terms of their subconscious and innate disposition, and there is no need for additional investigation, or proofing for this matter.

Necessity of certainty in Religion

The Third Matter: The necessity for a person to ascertain when it comes to matters of religion.

Given that one of the aspects of this clear intellectual cognition is the necessity for a person to exercise caution regarding potentially significant matters, it can generally be said, that the necessity for a person to exercise caution in matters of religion—or, in other words, concerning these great truths—relies on self-evident intellectual cognitions that form the structure of human life in all its actions. Neglecting this is not only a deviation from the clear principles of knowledge, but also a deviation from the clear principles of reason, as will be further clarified later.

Thus, every person who does not deceive themselves and sincerely seeks the truth must form a worldview for themselves by resolving these truths and reflecting on them—particularly considering what will be discussed later, which is that in the case of significant truths, the mere possibility of their validity is sufficient to warrant serious attention to them. This is especially the case if such a possibility exists prior to thorough investigation and examination. Based on this, no-one can reasonably turn away from sufficient verification of these truths, given their importance, unless they claim that their falsity is entirely evident without any need for research or verification. This is a clear gamble, which I do not believe anyone who respects their intellect and understands the implications of their words would commit.

Hence, it is hoped that those who come across this study do not treat it as intellectual luxury or rush to adopt a positive or negative stance towards it until they have sufficiently reflected on it and, with the aid of this study, formed for themselves a mature perspective regarding these truths.

Quranic Logic on Conviction

The Fourth Matter: Concerning oneself with the comparison of the logic of the Quran and innate intellectual reasoning when it comes to conviction.

Religion, in its effort to convince people, proceeds from a logic that it adopts and inherently follows. Therefore, we must reflect on the extent to which this logic aligns with innate intellectual reasoning (*al-manṭiq al-ʿaqlī al-fiṭrī*). This can be examined through observing the Quran, which, from a historical perspective, is the most authentic religious message presented to humanity from the Creator of this universe and life. Moreover, in terms of its content, it stands out as the most appropriate and remarkable in its teachings as a whole compared to other scriptures, to the extent that even some scholars of other religions have acknowledged its magnificence.

When examining the texts of the Glorious Quran, it becomes evident that its foundational approach to convincing people also relies on intellectual assent—both speculative and practical—aligning with the previously established self-evident principle that conviction must proceed from such reasoning.

As for its reliance on the speculative intellect (*al-'aql al-naẓarī*), then this is because we frequently observe in the verses of the Quran an emphasis on intellect and an effort to stimulate reflection, reasoning, and contemplation in various forms. This is achieved by drawing attention to the universe, examining its depths, and understanding the significations of created beings as signs pointing to what lies beyond them. It also involves comparing the content of the divine message presented with the standards of speculative reason. This is evident in the concluding remarks of many verses, following descriptions of the marvels of life, such as the statement of Allah, the Exalted: {*For a people who reason*}[1], and His statement: {*For a people who reflect*}[2].

It is well-known that this method of persuasion is rooted in stimulating and activating the intellect. In the sermon of the Commander of the Faithful (peace be upon him), there is an indication that the primary purpose of sending Prophets

---

1. See: *Sūrat al-Baqara*: 164, *al-Ra'd*: 4, *al-Naḥl*: 12, 67, *al-'Ankabūt*: 35, *al-Rūm*: 24, 28, *al-Jāthiya*: 5.
2. See: *Sūrat Yūnus*: 24, *al-Ra'd*: 3, *al-Naḥl*: 11, *al-Rūm*: 21, *al-Zumar*: 42, *al-Jāthiya*: 13.

is to awaken and motivate the intellect for comprehension. He said: *"He sent to them His Prophets in succession to fulfil the pledges of His creation, to remind them of His forgotten favours, to establish the truth by conveying His message, to revive their numbed intellects. He instructed [his Prophets] to show them the signs of His power: the roof of the sky above them raised high, the cradle of the earth beneath them spread wide, the means of livelihood that give them life, the appointed times of death that bring an end to them, the ailments that wear them out, and the successive events that befall them."*³

As for its emphasis on practical reason (*al-'aql al-'amalī*), this is evident in how the Quran obligates belief in Allah based on gratitude. Gratitude, as is known, is an ethical concept. Additionally, the Quran comprises the principles of what is right (*ma'rūf*) and evil (*munkar*) as the foundation of religious legislation. Moreover, it argues for the truthfulness of the Prophet (peace be upon him and his progeny) and the divine message he came with, by emphasising that its content includes enjoining good and forbidding evil. Good is that which people recognise through their intellects and find reassuring, while evil is what they reject and turn away from in their innate disposition. These are ethical concepts encompassing noble deeds and their opposites. Allah, the Exalted, said: {*Those who follow the Messenger, the gentile Prophet, whom they find described in the Torah and the Gospel*

---

3. See: *Nahj al-Balāgha*, pg. 43, Sermon 1. Edited by: Ṣubḥī al-Ṣāliḥ

that is with them, who commands them to do what is right and forbids them from what is evil}.[4]

Yes, there is no doubt that religion makes use of miracles to convince people. However, reliance was not placed solely on miracles; rather, their use in the Quran came in a secondary role. This is why we find, in many instances, that Allah, the Exalted, did not respond to the disbelievers' demands for miracles from the Prophet (peace be upon him and his progeny) as a condition for believing in his message. In some of these verses, there even appears to be a desire on the part of the Prophet (peace be upon him and his progeny) for an increase in miracles, as part of his effort to guide the people and out of his sorrow over their persistence in misguidance. Allah, the Exalted, said: {*And if their denial is unbearable, then seek a tunnel into the earth or a ladder to the sky, if you can, to bring them a sign. If Allah had willed, He would have brought them all together in guidance. So do not be among the ignorant.*}[5]

This is in addition to the fact that the evidentiary power of miracles also relies on the rational faculty, given that they are extraordinary acts beyond human capability, signifying a connection between the individual performing them and a superhuman power.

---

4. See: *Sūrat al-Aʿrāf*: 157.
5. See: *Sūrat al-Anʿām*: 35.

From all this, it becomes clear that the notion circulating in some circles that the logic of religion is based on reliance upon the evidentiary value of miracles and supernatural phenomena is incorrect. Rather, the primary reliance of religion—particularly Islam—is on stimulating the intellect, encouraging reflection on the content of religion, and awakening the spirit of contemplation and thought in human beings.

Thus, it is becomes manifest that divine religion, represented by Islam—which is the culmination and seal of all religions—proceeds from the same universal, innate intellectual foundation: the speculative intellect (*al-'aql al-naẓarī*) in its clear inferences, and practical reason (*al-'aql al-'amalī*) from what is witnessed by a human through their pure and uncorrupted innate disposition.

If there are aspects of religious teachings that some people believe to contradict the rational faculty, it is necessary to ascertain whether religion provides an interpretation or explanation for them, given its insistence that the rational faculty and rationality are its foundation and the basis of its method of conviction.

Research Methodology and Overview

The Fifth Matter: This research is divided into five sections.

The First Section: Pertains to the essence of religion.

It includes a discussion on the content of religion according to its teachings and texts, based on the premise that verifying any belief requires accurate and reliable analysis of its foundations, components, and principles.

This section demonstrates that religion comprises epistemological, cosmological, humanistic, and legislative perspectives. The epistemological perspective reminds us of the broad outlines of a sound and accurate epistemological methodology. The cosmological perspective establishes the existence of Allah, His attributes, and His regulating of affairs. The humanistic perspective addresses Allah's care for humanity and the continuation of human existence beyond this life. As for the legislative perspective, it highlights the natural law and its complementary legislative rulings.

The Second Section: Pertains to the direction of religion in human life.

This section also aims to clarify another significant aspect of religion, namely its orientation toward critical and vital matters. In essence, it serves as a continuation of the first section.

It includes several themes, each addressing a key dimension of human life and outlining the direction of religion concerning it, such as general rationality, knowledge, inspiration, wisdom, ethics, happiness, personal freedom, and others.

The Third Section: Pertains to the necessity of religious knowledge for every mature individual.

It includes a discussion on the general standard for the necessity of verification concerning various matters. It examines why we focus on certain things in our practical lives while disregarding others, posing the question: What is the equation that drives us in this regard?

We explained that this equation is threefold, based on the degree of cognition, the significance of what is perceived, and the level of care that must be devoted to it. In light of this, we explored the implications of this equation concerning religion and observed that it necessitates deep attention to verifying the truth of religion, as it is the most critical issue in a person's life.

The Fourth Section: Pertains to sound general principles that should guide religious knowledge.

This section encompasses the general principles of human and religious knowledge, which a sound-minded individual naturally and innately adheres to. In reality, these principles represent the innate logic of humanity and the logic underlying belief in religion. Since humans are prone to error in understanding these principles or in their application, it becomes necessary to define and clarify them in order to safeguard their cognition from mistakes, especially in this critical matter—the matter of religion.

The necessity of this clarification is further emphasised when considering that resolving the great truths of life, which form the essence of religion, is not an area where emulation (*taqlīd*) is appropriate; rather, it must be based on sound reasoning and mature evidence.

The Fifth Section: Is a brief examination of the three greater truths that form the essence of religion: the existence of Allah, His message to humanity, and the continuation of human existence after this life.

Thus, this series is divided into five independent yet interrelated sections, each addressing an aspect essential for gaining clarity and insight.

We have taken care to ensure that the content and presentation of this study are accessible, clear, and straightforward, avoiding the obscurity of scientific and technical jargon where simpler expressions can be used. This approach follows the method we observed in religion—as represented in the Quran—which directs its discourse to the general public in an easy and clear language, while maintaining sound reasoning and objectivity in persuasion and conviction.

I urge the readers to dedicate themselves to following this study and engaging with it as they seek the truth of religion, so they may attain clarity in this critical matter, which is undoubtedly the most consequential issue in a person's life.

And with this, we begin the discussion on "the essence of religion".

THE ESSENCE OF
RELIGION

Religion as a Defined Perspective

1. Religion—in its sense that commands human attention by means of their innate disposition—is a worldview based on two fundamental principles:

Firstly: The existence of a Creator for this universe and its beings, a Creator who is concerned with all creation in general and humanity in particular, as evidenced through His message sent to humankind.

Secondly: The recognition that humans are not merely material beings who cease to exist upon death, as might appear to be the case with other living creatures. Instead, humans are eternal beings, and death is merely a stage in their existence, during which their soul separates from their body, only to return to it at a later time. Furthermore, their happiness or misery in that subsequent phase is determined by their deeds in this worldly life: {*So whoever does an atom's* *weight of good will see it ✽ and whoever does an atom's weight of evil will see it*}.⁶

Two Alternative Worldviews

2. In contrast to this religious worldview, there are two other perspectives...

The First: Asserts that humans are left to themselves, without any special care in their creation or any continuation after their death. According to this view, the consequences of human actions are confined to what they experience in this life—whether in terms of their own feelings and behaviour or the positive and negative reactions of others. Beyond this, no greater reality exists. That is with regards to the human being.

As for the Creator of existence, the universe, and life, this perspective is divided into two directions:

> **The First Direction**—commonly known as atheism—denies the very existence of a Creator. It claims that matter is eternal and that its transformations over a long period gave rise to the universe and all life within it. This notion is reflected in the statement of some disbelievers mentioned in the Quran: {*Nothing but time destroys us*}.⁷

---

6. See: *Sūrat al-Zalzala*: 7-8.
7. See: *Sūrat al-Jāthiya*: 24.

The Second Direction—commonly referred to as deism—acknowledges the existence of a non-material Creator of life. However, it holds that this Creator is not concerned with humanity in terms of guidance, care, interaction, or compassion. According to this view, humans—like other living and non-living entities—were created according to certain laws and systems that they are left to follow without further intervention.

The Second: Commonly known as agnosticism—this perspective adopts hesitation and indecision regarding the truth of life, its origins, and humanity's place within it. It neither affirms nor denies these realities, thus leaving open the possibility that the religious worldview is correct, as well as the possibility of atheistic or deistic perspectives being valid.

At first glance, one might assume that this agnostic perspective, in practical terms, leads to the same outcomes as the previous perspectives—namely atheism or deism—since doubt and possibility alone do not seem to produce any tangible effects.

However, it will later become clear that this is not the case. In fact, even if this perspective arises after extensive investigation and examination, it is still obligated to act upon the potential implications of the religious worldview. This includes considering the possibility of a Creator who is concerned with humanity, and the possibility that human actions are the foundations of happiness or misery in another world. The significance of these possibilities rationally necessitates acting upon them, according to a self-evident rational equation that will be explained further.

Impact of Diverging Worldviews

3. These perspectives—the religious worldview and the two alternative views—have profound effects on human life in terms of its orientations, motivations, and legislations.

From the standpoint of the religious worldview, human life is purposeful. Humanity is given the choice between two paths: the path of knowledge and virtue, and the path of ignorance and vice. A person's actions carry deep significance in shaping and building their character in a sound manner. Every individual will take their place tomorrow, as every soul will be recompensed for what it earned and held accountable for what it acquired. Thus, whoever commits evil will not escape its consequences, and whoever does good will not be deprived of its effects. Those who endure imposed hardships will have them counted in their favour. Furthermore, Allah, the Exalted, serves as a supporter for those who believe in Him, trust in Him, and take Him as their guardian. Humans are journeying toward another life, as this world is a means, not an end; a passageway, not a dwelling place.

On the other hand, from the perspective of the two alternative views, this life is the ultimate goal. It becomes akin to a gamble: those who succeed in achieving pleasures—even at the expense of others, provided they escape worldly punishment—find happiness, while those who are overpowered or afflicted with trials suffer misery. Some proponents of these views argue that humans are not free in their actions but are driven by necessity, much like other animals.

Dimensions of Religious Worldview

4. It is essential to outline the features of the religious worldview and its key principles to build upon them in subsequent discussions, particularly in determining the appropriate attention it deserves and the proper methods of verification.

This clarification helps place everything in its proper context, distinguishing the fundamental and definitive principles of religion from matters of application, interpretation, or secondary derivation. This ensures that religion is understood clearly and distinctly, without being obscured by details of implementation or differences in *ijtihād*.

When viewed through its dimensions, the religious worldview can be broken down into multiple interrelated and complementary perspectives: on knowledge, the universe, humanity, and legislation.

1. The religious epistemological perspective reflects the view of religion regarding the proper, sound, and rational methodology for acquiring knowledge, its general tools, and its accessible limits.

2. The religious cosmological perspective represents the explanation religion provides concerning the dimensions of existence and the universe, including the affirmation of a wise Creator and His governance of the universe and all its beings.

3. The religious anthropological perspective elaborates on the reality of humanity, highlighting human capacities and potentials such as intellect, conscience, emotions, and free-will. It also affirms the continuation of human existence beyond this life and emphasises the Creator's care and attention toward humanity.

4. The religious legislative perspective includes the principles of legislation that align with the psychological and physical constitution of humans and the innate nature upon which they were created.

Religion as a Defined Perspective

Religious Epistemology

The first perspective: Is the religious epistemological perspective, which comprises several matters.

Value of Human Cognition

The First Matter: Is that the religious epistemological perspective acknowledges the validity of human cognition in its certainties, namely, areas where the judgement of reason is clear and unambiguous, accessible to any person with sound thinking.

However, it also holds that humans—despite this—cannot entirely dispense themselves of epistemological support in their understanding of the universe. This is due to two reasons:

One of them: Is that humans, through certain inner feelings and contemplation of the material world, its wonders, and its organisation, may uncover signs of a hidden Creator who made the universe, however, most people do so only with difficulty, or without reaching certitude. Often, such discoveries are vague and entangled with myths and superstitions, as seen in practices like the worship of planets, stars, individuals, and idols.

Whilst the other: Is that certain significant and critical truths are fundamentally inaccessible to human cognition, such as the concept of another future realm, the return of humans to life, and their eternal existence from thereon.

Forms of Epistemological Support

The Second Matter: Is that the epistemological support provided to humans in religion is of four types.

1. Affirming what human reason already discerns, in opposition to myths and superstitions. An example of this is found in the Quran's emphasis on rational judgments that reject the suitability of idols, celestial bodies, or individuals for divinity. Regarding idols, the Quran highlights their being man-made, stating: {*He said, 'Do you worship what you carve [with your own hands], * when it is Allah who created you and your handiwork?'*}.[8]

Concerning the deification of ʿĪsā b. Maryam (peace be upon him), the Quran says: {*The Messiah, the son of Maryam, was not but a Messenger; [other] Messengers have passed on before*

---

8. See: *Sūrat al-Ṣāffāt*: 95-96.

*him. And his mother was a supporter of truth. They both used to eat food. See how We make the signs clear to them; then see how they are deluded}.*⁹ This verse indicates that someone with such human traits cannot—according to clear rational cognition—be considered a deity.

Similarly, regarding the worship of celestial bodies, the Quran notes the fact they are subjugated entities of transient nature. They appear at times and disappear at others, making it inconceivable for them to be the Creator or Governor of the universe. The Quran states: {*When the night covered him (i.e. Ibrāhīm), he saw a star. He said, 'This is my Lord.' But when it set, he said, 'I do not like things that set.'* ✻ *And when he saw the moon rising, he said, 'This is my Lord.' But when it set, he said, 'Unless my Lord guides me, I will surely be among the people who have gone astray.'* ✻ *And when he saw the sun rising, he said, 'This is my Lord; this is greater!' But when it set, he said, 'O my people, indeed I am free from all you associate with Allah'*}.¹⁰

2. Alerting and awakening humans to matters they observe and witness but do not fully comprehend or derive their significations and conclusions. This refers to drawing attention to realities that, when pointed out, awaken individuals from their heedlessness and redirects their thoughts toward their implications. Often, a person may

---

9. See: *Sūrat al-Mā'ida*: 75.
10. See: *Sūrat al-An'ām*: 76-78.

marvel at how they had observed these realities without recognising their implications.

An example of this is the Quran's emphasis on the signs of creation and the order of the universe as evidence of the Creator. While these signs can be perceived independently by individuals, they may fail to fully grasp their significance without guidance. In such cases, they require someone to draw their attention to these realities and their meanings.[11]

3. Informing humans of what they are unaware of, but need regarding matters of the metaphysical realm. This includes concepts such as the Hereafter, where it would be difficult for humans to clearly and definitively derive the existence of a resurrection and a next life without revelation.[12]

---

11. The reason for human heedlessness regarding the implications of certain matters—as will be discussed later when discussing principles of cognitive verification—lies in psychological factors. Among the most significant of these is the diminishing of the indicative power of something beyond itself due to habituation. When a person becomes accustomed to something, they tend to overlook its implications.

12. It is possible that certain human emotions serve as a prelude for such news to be accepted within oneself, despite its being beyond the reach of their cognitive ability. Among these emotions is the innate human love for existence and desire for immortality. However, it is challenging for a person to develop and crystallise such feelings into a state of complete and clear cognition.

4. Informing humans of their inability to delve deeply into the metaphysical realm using their intellect alone. This is due to the absence of clear tools available to humans for such inquiries and the invalidity of comparing the metaphysical world to the material world.

When humans delve deeply into thinking about the metaphysical realm, theorising about it, and building upon such ideas, they do not arrive at clear conclusions. Instead, they often end up embracing false superstitions, such as the Greek belief in the existence of "Ten Intellects (*al-ʿUqūl al-ʿAshara*)" intermediating between the Creator and the material world. Similarly, some believed in the existence of a supreme being for each type of creature, responsible for managing its affairs, which they referred to as "Lords of Species (*Arbāb al-Anwāʿ*)." Others, like the polytheists of the pre-Islamic era, held the belief that angels were "daughters" of God, or similar erroneous notions.[13]

Respect for Human Reason

It thus becomes clear that the religious epistemological perspective respects human reason in its certainties and

---

13. It is noteworthy that the four aforementioned forms of epistemological support provided by religion apply not only to the cosmological perspective but also to its view of humanity and sound legislation, as will be further explained in the discussion on the legislative dimension.

unequivocal judgments—those areas of cognition that are clear and readily accessible to the intellect. However, from the standpoint of religion, human understanding alone is insufficient to reveal the complete picture of the universe, its dimensions, and the significant truths it contains. This stands in contrast to certain philosophical schools of thought within Muslim circles, which claim that humans can fully comprehend the entirety of existence and its mysteries through contemplation and inquiry.

In reality, the arguments presented in this regard—which proponents of the aforementioned school consider to be sound proofs—are, in essence, no more than mere mental preferences or ad-hoc assumptions of implausibility that are rooted in one's inclinations, aversions, or astonishment. These are often framed in an artistic manner, giving them the appearance of rigorous proof.

Two Pillars: Intellection and Devotion

The Third Matter: Which stems from the above—is that the religious epistemological perspective relies on two fundamental pillars: intellection and devotion...

Intellection operates in the domain of clear cognitive understanding, while devotion pertains to those matters beyond human cognition; issues that fall within the grey area, where human intellect cannot provide a definitive answer.

Whoever extends rationality beyond the domains that reason is capable of comprehending falls into illusion and confusion. Likewise, whoever extends devotion into domains that reason is capable of understanding falls into error or superstition. But whoever assigns each to its proper place and adheres to it accordingly has struck the mark.

Relying on devotion in its appropriate domains is not a diminishment of human cognition. Rather, it is a realistic acknowledgment of the limitations of human cognition, reminding individuals of the areas where their intellectual faculties fall short.

This principle is alluded to in numerous religious texts, including the verse in *Sūrat Āl 'Imrān* that divides the verses of the Quran into *muḥkamāt* (clear) and *mutashābihāt* (obscure). As Allah, the Exalted says: {*It is He who has sent down to you the Book. In it are verses that are clear—these are the cornerstone of the Book—and others obscure. As for those in whose hearts is deviation, they will follow that of it which is ambiguous, seeking discord and seeking its fulfilment. And no-one knows its fulfilment except Allah. But those firm in knowledge say, 'We believe in it; all of it is from our Lord.' And no-one will take heed except those of understanding*}.[14]

---

14. See: *Sūrat Āl 'Imrān*: 7. And, God-Willing, further details and clarification on this discussion will follow in the fourth section.

The *muḥkamāt* are the clear and unequivocal verses where no room for doubt exists concerning their truthfulness based on initial objections. The *mutashābihāt* are those verses where doubt or difficulty may arise, such as the foretelling of resurrection and the Day of Judgment, which some reject based on arguments like: {*They say, 'When we have become bones and dust, will we really be resurrected as a new creation?'*}.[15]

The term *ta'wīl* (fulfilment) refers to the eventual reality that confirms the truthfulness of what has been foretold, as Allah, the Exalted says: {*Are they waiting except for its fulfilment? The Day its fulfilment comes, those who had ignored it before will say, 'The Messengers of our Lord had come with the truth, so are there any intercessors to intercede for us, or could we be sent back to do other than what we used to do?' They will have lost themselves, and whatever they used to invent will have departed from them*}.[16]

Divine Assistance for Creation

The Fourth Matter: The divine assistance provided to creation came through the sending of a message to clarify the correct and comprehensive perspective on existence, the universe, and the human being.

---

15. See: *Sūrat al-Isrā'*: 49.
16. See: *Sūrat al-A'rāf*: 53.

To deliver this message to creation, Allah chose individuals from among the people themselves. These individuals were characterised by sound intellect, clear understanding, moderation in behaviour, purity of disposition, a love for truth and virtue, steadfastness in the face of challenges, and compassion for others. They exhibited no traits that would compromise their mental integrity, no ambition for social dominance, and no tendencies toward cunning, deceit, or manipulation.

Revelation was sent to them in a clear and distinct manner, possessing attributes and qualities—both in scope and nature—that far exceeded what could be imagined by humans as hallucinations or disturbances arising from psychological issues.

Furthermore, Allah supported them with miracles that, in their scope and nature, required superhuman abilities far beyond anything familiar to humanity, such as the actions of sorcerers, soothsayers, and their ilk. These miracles differed fundamentally from such phenomena, both in scope and nature.

The individuals chosen for this message were already known within their communities, and their behaviour, abilities, and inclinations had been closely observed by those around them over an extended period. No evidence existed of them engaging in peculiar claims or unusual conduct.

Their proofs emerged within societies familiar with false claims, ensuring that their message could not be dismissed as something similar. This allowed the ultimate proof of the truthfulness of the Messenger's claim to be established for all creation.

When a period passed, during which the clarity of the message gradually diminished, Allah sent another Messenger to re-establish the proof and dispel ambiguities and doubts. The last of His Messengers was Prophet Muḥammad (peace be upon him and his progeny), through whom Allah facilitated the preservation of His message in His Noble Book—a message for all of creation—ensuring its historical preservation with undeniable clarity.

Allah (Glorified is He) chose to send His Messengers to societies that were most characterised by extremism, arrogance, and oppression so that the message could reach other societies through the general laws of human interaction.

Thus, these Messengers became the intermediaries between the Creator and humanity, clarifying the outline and horizons of life as designed by its Creator. They guided humanity toward knowledge, reason, wisdom, justice, and purification, as Allah says: {*It is He who has sent among the gentiles a Messenger from themselves, reciting to them His verses, purifying them, and teaching them the Book and wisdom*}.[17] And He said: {*We sent*

---

17. See: *Sūrat al-Jumʿa*: 2.

Our Messengers with clear proofs and sent down with them the Scripture and the Balance so that the people may administer justice}.[18]

---

18. See: *Sūrat al-Ḥadīd*: 25.

Religious Cosmology

As for the second perspective—among the varying religious views on existence—is the perspective of religion concerning existence and the universe. This perspective revolves around a critically important topic: The existence of the Creator of life, along with His attributes and actions.

According to the religious perspective, humans perceive in the material world and its entities a clear indication of an unseen Being, and they find evidence of His attributes of perfection, such as power, knowledge, and creative capacity (*ibdāʿ*). In affirming, elaborating, and assisting humanity in understanding this perspective, religion highlights three key truths:

The First: The existence of a Creator for the universe and life.

The Second: That this Creator regulates the affairs of the universe and all its beings.

The Third: That He has a special concern for humanity.

Here, we will discuss the first two truths[19]...

Truths of the Creator

As for the first truth: Which is the fact that Allah is the Creator of the universe and life, then this—according to the religious perspective—encompasses several aspects.

Existence of the Creator

The First Matter: A Creator exists for humanity, for all beings, and laid down laws and regulations, which He can be discovered through. This can also be done by observing their design, how they are fashioned, their origination, and their changing nature. Many verses in the Quran point to this, such as: {*Were they created by nothing, or are they the creators [of themselves]?*}[20]

Creator's Attributes: Life, Power, Knowledge

The Second Matter: Is that Allah, the Exalted, is characterised by eternal life, all-encompassing power, and comprehensive

---

19. The third truth will be addressed later in the discussion on the religious perspective regarding "The Creator's Care for Humanity."
20. See: *Sūrat al-Ṭūr*: 35, as well as numerous other verses in chapters such as *al-Rūm*: 20–25, *Fuṣṣilat*: 37, 39, *al-Shūrā*: 29, 32, *al-Naḥl*: 11, *al-Shuʿarāʾ*: 8, *al-ʿAnkabūt*: 44, *al-Aʿrāf*: 54, *al-Raʿd*: 2, and *Ghāfir*: 64.

knowledge. The grandeur of the universe and its beings testifies to this, making it valid to say that Allah's greatness, power, and knowledge surpass what humans can conceive or imagine, as indicated by various Quranic verses.

The truth and depth of this meaning become clearer over time as new dimensions of Allah's power are unveiled. Examples include the profound temporal depth of the universe, the vastness of space with its thousands of galaxies—each containing millions of stars—and the complex laws governing life and its phenomena, particularly in the realm of physics. These reveal an astonishing harmony in the universe, which continues to amaze even the most brilliant scientists. Furthermore, discoveries in this field have not ceased and seem unlikely to ever come to an end.

Thus, it is natural for humans to be unable to comprehend the full scope of what Allah's power entails, especially regarding matters they have not yet witnessed; which should have been priorly accepted after revelation on the matter.

A critical mistake in this regard is the tendency of some schools of thought to consider the unfamiliarity or strangeness of certain religious concepts and rulings as a prior indicator of their falsehood. For example, rejecting the idea that Allah can resurrect humans after their death for another life is akin to someone marvelling at an extraordinary creation they admire and then denying the possibility of another, equally wondrous creation, assuming that what they have seen represents the pinnacle of craftsmanship in its field.

Creator's Wisdom

The Third Matter: Is that Allah is wise in His actions. His wisdom can be understood as follows:

Firstly: Allah has created a harmonious universe, with all its parts in proportion and balance. This is observable to us and affirmed by physicists, who emphasise the astonishing consistency of all the laws governing the material universe. This coherence reflects Allah's supreme wisdom, placing all things in their appropriate positions and ensuring their alignment.

Someone characterised by such wisdom does not act inconsistently—for instance, forgiving the sins of some individuals while excluding others, or granting to some while withholding from others, despite their equality in status and circumstances, without any justifiable preference.

Secondly: Allah does not act frivolously or without purpose. Instead, His actions are deliberate, wise, and perfectly aligned with meaningful and appropriate objectives. As He says: {*And We did not create the heavens and the earth and what is between them in play. * We did not create them except in truth, but most of them do not know*}.[21]

---

21. See: *Sūrat al-Dukhān*: 38-39.

Purpose of Creation

The Fourth Matter: Is that one of the Creator's goals in creating this material world and establishing its laws is as follows:

Firstly: To manifest His power and demonstrate His greatness to the rational beings among His creation, who, through reflection and contemplation, can grasp the dimensions and horizons of this world. This can be likened—though Allah's example is far greater—to an artist painting a masterpiece or sculpting a magnificent sculpture to showcase their artistic ability.

Secondly: To prepare for another existence, which is the ultimate goal toward which the material universe and its beings are moving. Without this next life, existence would seem meaningless.[22]

---

22. This purpose aligns with findings in modern science, which assert that every entity in the universe has a goal toward which it moves according to the laws of existence that define its creation. For instance, biology illustrates how every animal is equipped with tools, instincts, and mechanisms enabling it to survive, reproduce, and protect itself from threats. When biologists analyse the features of a creature—such as its beak, wings, or other characteristics—
they explain how these traits align with the animal's survival, propagation, and preservation. This notion is also reflected in the Quran, where Allah says: {*Our Lord is He who gave each thing its form and then guided it*}. See: *Sūrat Ṭa-Hā*: 50.

Allah says: {*The Day when We will roll up the skies like a written scroll. We shall reproduce creation just as We produced it the first time—a promise binding upon Us. Indeed, We will do it*}.[23] And He (Glorified is He) said: {*The Day the earth will be replaced by another earth, and the heavens [as well], and they will come out before Allah, the One, the Subduer*}[24] and other such verses that indicate the same thing.

Allah (Glorified is He) mentions that believers discern this ultimate goal through their reflection on the creation of the heavens and the earth, as stated in His words: {*And they reflect on the creation of the heavens and the earth, [they say], 'Our Lord, You did not create this frivolously; You are exalted [from such a thing]; so protect us from the torment of the Fire*}.[25]

This grand transformation of the universe is described in various verses, such as: {*When the sun is shrouded [in darkness]*}[26] and His statement: {*When the sky is rent asunder*}.[27]

This ultimate goal of the universe underscores the centrality of human-beings in this life, as humans are the focal point of what will unfold in the Hereafter. This is illustrated in *Sūrat al-Takwīr* following the vivid imagery of the next creation, where

---

23. See: *Sūrat al-Anbiyāʾ*: 104.
24. See: *Sūrat Ibrāhīm*: 48.
25. See: *Sūrat Āl ʿImrān*: 191.
26. See: *Sūrat al-Takwīr*: 1.
27. See: *Sūrat al-Inshiqāq*: 1.

Allah says: {*And when the female infant [who was buried alive] is asked, * for what sin she was killed, * and when the scrolls [of deeds] are laid open, * and when the sky is stripped away, * and when Hellfire is fiercely set ablaze, * and when Paradise is brought near, * a soul will [then] know what it has brought about*}.[28] Similarly, in *Sūrat al-Inshiqāq*, after a depiction of this event, Allah addresses humanity directly: {*O mankind, indeed you are labouring toward your Lord with [great] exertion and will meet it[s consequences]. * So as for he who is given his record in his right hand, he will have an easy reckoning*}.[29]

Creator as a Non-Material Being

The Fifth Matter: The Creator is a non-material existence. The rational mind clearly indicates that none of the entities perceptible to human senses—whether humans, animals, trees, or inanimate objects—can possess divinity. These entities are products of the laws governing existence and life, much like their counterparts in nature. They are unfit to dominate the universe, with all its antiquity, vastness, and precision. This is emphasised in the noble Quranic verses, such as: {*He said, 'Do you worship what you carve [with your own hands], * when it is Allah who created you and your handiwork?'*}[30]

---

28. See: *Sūrat al-Takwīr*: 8-14.
29. See: *Sūrat al-Inshiqāq*: 6-8.
30. See: *Sūrat al-Ṣāffāt*: 95-96.

From this, it follows that Allah's nature is of a transcendent kind, far above the attributes and limitations of material existence. He is free from growth, deficiency, and division in His essence, unlike what is observed in the material world. This concept is repeatedly emphasised in religious texts, whether in the Quranic verses or in the sermons of *Nahj al-Balāgha*.

Unity of the Creator

The Sixth Matter: The Creator of life is One. There is no trace of a multiplicity of creators of the universe or its beings. Everything operates within a unified system, governed by consistent laws. If there were multiple deities, it would inevitably lead to conflict in their governance of the universe, as stated in the Quran: {*Had there been within them [i.e. the heavens and the earth] gods besides Allah, they both would have been ruined*}.[31] Moreover, if other gods existed, they would have sent their own Messengers, as Allah has sent His, as noted by the Commander of the Faithful (peace be upon him) in his advice to his son, al-Ḥasan (peace be upon him): *"If your Lord had a partner, his Messengers would have come to you."*[32]

---

31. See: *Sūrat al-Anbiyā'*: 22.
32. *Nahj al-Balāgha*, pg. 396, Aphorism 31.

Limits of Human Comprehension

The Seventh Matter: Allah, the Exalted, is far greater than human comprehension of the details of His essence or to be subject to description, unlike the way created beings and their attributes can be described. This is evident given that He is not a material existence. Humans cannot grasp the nature of His essence or its characteristics due to their lack of the necessary tools to do so. Consequently, reflecting or theorising about His essence becomes futile.[33]

It thus follows: That it is a grave error to deduce the nature of His perfect attributes—such as His knowledge—based on the attributes of His creation. As stated in the Quranic verse: {*There is nothing like unto Him*}.[34] His essence bears no resemblance to the attributes of other beings, nor to the manner in which their characteristics are defined.[35]

---

33. Some movements in Ṣūfism and theoretical mysticism, as well as some philosophical movements, have attempted to theorise about this matter. These attempts are closer to delusions than reality.
34. See: *Sūrat al-Shūrā*: 11.
35. The Commander of the Faithful (peace be upon him), elaborated on this issue in several sermons that can be found in *Nahj al-Balāgha*, addressing the distinct nature of Allah's attributes compared to those of His creation. Numerous traditions widely transmitted in the hadith collections of the Imams from the Ahl al-Bayt also caution against contemplating on the essence of Allah (Blessed and Exalted is He).

Creator as the Universe's Regulator

As for the second truth concerning the Creator: —His role as the Regulator of the universe and all beings—encompasses several matters, including...

Sustaining the Universe

The First Matter: Allah, the Exalted, continually bestows existence upon the universe and its beings, guiding them toward their goals. The existence and attributes of these beings are not self-sustaining; rather, their existence and continuity depend on His constant support. Allah says: {*Indeed, Allah keeps heavens and the earth from ceasing [to exist]. And if they should cease, no-one could stop them other than Him*}.[36] Similarly, their removal and annihilation rest entirely in His hands, occurring whenever and however He wills. The relationship of these beings to Allah can be likened to energy, which requires constant supply from its generating source.

This concept is not negated by reason. Although reason cannot grasp how things derive continuity in their existence from Allah (Glorified is He), the inability to comprehend something does not equate to its denial. This is especially evident in our own experience of being unaware of the essence of many phenomena that we nonetheless affirm

---

36. See: *Sūrat al-Fāṭir*: 41.

through their effects. For example, we know that gravity causes objects to fall, but the true nature and essence of gravity remain beyond our understanding. The same applies to other discovered elements and forces. This reality has been acknowledged by prominent natural scientists, as reflected in Allah's words: {*And you have only been given a little knowledge*}.[37]

This view stands in contrast to the claim of those who believe that Allah created beings according to specific laws and then entrusted them entirely to those laws, with no ongoing involvement in their continuity or continuance.

Divine Authority Over Creation

The Second Matter: Allah, the Exalted, holds authority over all the affairs of creation; thus, He is able to act upon them contrary to their usual behaviour. This occurs in two ways.

The first is through a clear disruption of natural laws, which is referred to as a miracle or extraordinary event. Examples of this include the birth of ʿĪsā b. Maryam (peace be upon him) without a father, the parting of the sea for Mūsā (peace be upon him), and the fire becoming a place of coolness and safety for Ibrāhīm (peace be upon him).

The second is by guiding external natural or psychological factors toward specific directions they would not otherwise

---

37. See: *Sūrat al-Isrāʾ*: 85.

take without divine intervention. For instance, directing rain clouds to barren lands in response to people's prayers for rain (Ṣalāt al-Istisqāʾ), or inspiring the mother of Mūsā (peace be upon him) to cast him into the river, which ultimately resulted in the preservation of her son and his return to her.

Throughout history, most people, regardless of their religious traditions, have turned to the Creator during times of distress and hardship, hoping He would relieve their afflictions through the channels and means He alone controls and directs as He wills.[38]

Gradual Creation of the Universe

The Third Matter: Allah (Glorified is He) did not create the universe and its beings all at once in their observed forms. Instead, His system of creation operates on the basis of first bringing things into existence in an initial state according to certain laws, and then developing them through those laws until they reach their intended goals.

This can be seen in the creation of humans, who begin as a fertilised drop of fluid, then grow into an embryo, and continue to develop until fully formed and equipped with the tools needed for life at birth.

---

38. This matter may be connected to the first point, considering that things are inherently linked to the divine will through their inner realities.

Similarly, the creation of the heavens and the earth is described in the Glorious Quran as occurring over six days.[39] Here, the term "day (*yawm*)" refers to phases of time or stages, as has been found in the usages of the Arabs,[40] and these periods may be exceedingly long, as indicated in the verse: {*Indeed, a day with your Lord is like a thousand years of those which you count*}.[41] Thus, the six days likely represent successive stages marked by significant cosmic events.

This gradual process of creation—starting with something seemingly insignificant and developing it according

---

39. See: *Sūrat al-Aʿrāf*: 54, *Yūnus*: 3, *Hūd*: 7, and other verses.
40. This usage is common; as the term "day (*yawm*)" often refers to the entire period during which a particular event occurred. For instance, it is said: "The Day of Badr," "The Day of Uḥud," "The Day of Ṣiffīn," and "The Day of the Camel." Allah also states: {*On the Day of Ḥunayn, when your great numbers pleased you, but they did not avail you at all, and the earth, despite its vastness, constrained you; then you turned back, fleeing*}.See: *Sūrat al-Tawba*: 25. Similarly, expressions like "the Last Day (*al-yawm al-ākhir*)" and "the Day of Resurrection (*yawm al-qiyāma*)" use the term in this manner. This is also reflected in the proverb: "The Day of Ḥalīma is not hidden." [Translator's note]: This is used as a proverb in Arabic to refer to any event that is widely known and famous. The phrase originates from the story of Ḥalīma bt. al-Ḥārith Jabala, whose father sent an army to fight al-Mundhir b. Māʾ al-Samāʾ. On that day, she provided perfume and incense to the troops, and the smoke of the incense rose so high it obscured the sun, making it one of the most renowned days in Arab history.
41. See: *Sūrat al-Ḥajj*: 47.

to intricate laws into something remarkable—could demonstrate an even greater capacity for ingenuity. For example, a person may directly lift a heavy object, or they may design a mechanical crane capable of doing so. The latter is a far more impressive display of ability. Accordingly, the Quran emphasises Allah's ability to produce extraordinary and perfected creations from simple beginnings, as stated: {*He who perfected everything He created and began the creation of man from clay. ∗ Then He made his descendants from an extract of humble fluid*}.[42]

---

42. See: *Sūrat al-Sajda*: 7-8.

Religious Cosmology

Religious Anthropology

As for the third perspective—in terms of religious view of the universe—pertains to humanity and encompasses two dimensions:

One of them: Is the Creator's special care for humanity.

While the Other: Is the reality of humanity and its existential dimensions.

Divine Care for Humanity

As for the first dimension, the religious perspective affirms that the Creator of the universe has a unique care for humanity. This is because humans, among all material beings, possess intellect and free-will. They can comprehend this material life and its laws, and are also able to uncover its secrets and mysteries, thus utilising and enjoying it. Therefore, they can be addressed and taught by Allah, the Exalted. Moreover, humans are capable of perceiving the existence of the Creator through the effects of His craftsmanship and creativity, which they are able to observe. They are also endowed with a conscience, enabling them to appreciate divine blessings and express gratitude, praise, and courtesy.

This divine care, as understood in the religious perspective, is expressed through multiple manifestations...

Humanity as the Creator's Steward

The First Manifestation: Is His consideration of humans as His stewards on earth, as expressed in the Quran: {*And [mention] when your Lord said to the angels, 'Indeed, I will place a steward upon the earth'*}.[43] It is almost as if this is with regards to humanity's endowment with the ability to choose and act freely, as well as the capacity to understand the laws of the universe and the nature of its beings. Through this, humans are elevated as the most noble and superior beings on the face of the Earth. Humanity is thus entrusted with comprehending Allah's (Glorified is He) power and creativity manifested in the creation of the universe and its laws. This truth has been acknowledged by a number of natural scientists.

---

43. See: *Sūrat al-Baqara*: 30.

Universe Prepared for Humanity

The Second Manifestation: Is the universe's preparation to accommodate humanity and its subjugation to human needs. This is by virtue of the fact that humanity was created after the earth and its surroundings, as well as plants, animals, minerals, and all other components of this life. Allah created these as a supportive environment for humans, akin to how parents prepare certain necessities to welcome a newborn. The Quran highlights this care, stating: {*Do you not see that Allah has subjected to you whatever is in the heavens and whatever is in the earth?*}[44] And He said: {*It is He who created for you all of that which is on the earth*}.[45]

Likewise, Allah (Glorified is He) has subjected all the beings surrounding humanity to its benefit, including the sun, moon, stars, plants, and animals. Humanity is the primary recipient of these creations, as many of these blessings—such as minerals and compounds—are specifically utilised and comprehended by humans for crafting tools and countless other applications.

Even beings that benefit other creatures, such as plants and animals, reflect humanity's centrality. The hegemony and dominance humans possess as the most advanced of creations, and their ability to optimise the use of these

---

44. See: *Sūrat Luqmān*: 20.
45. See: *Sūrat al-Baqara*: 29.

resources, signify that humanity is the primary purpose of their existence.

Divine Care from Inception

The Third Manifestation: Is the association of humanity's reation with direct instruction, guidance, and honour. This is evident in the story of Adam's creation, as Allah says: {*And [mention] when your Lord said to the angels, 'Indeed, I will place a steward upon the earth.' They said, 'Will You place upon it one who causes corruption therein and sheds blood, while we exalt You with praise and sanctify You?' He said, 'Indeed, I know that which you do not know.' * And He taught Adam the names—all of them. Then He presented them to the angels and said, 'Inform Me of the names of these, if you are truthful.' * They said, 'Exalted are You; we have no knowledge except what You have taught us. Indeed, it is You who is the Knowing, the Wise.' * He said, 'O Adam, inform them of their names.' And when he had informed them of their names, He said, 'Did I not tell you that I know the unseen [aspects] of the heavens and the earth? And I know what you reveal and what you conceal.'*}[46]

Allah's Grace (*Lutf*) Toward Humanity

The Fourth Manifestation: Is the grace of Allah, the Exalted, toward humanity and His assistance in their times of need. When humans ask of Him, He provides; when they call upon

---

46. See: *Sūrat al-Baqara*: 30-33.

Him, He responds; and when they seek His help, He aids them. He may even assist them in times of distress without humans explicitly asking or praying.

This grace is manifested in two forms...

The First: Is Manifest Grace (*al-Lutf al-Ẓāhir*), which is openly displayed through the disruption of life's natural laws by means of clear miracles and extraordinary events. This is akin to that which has proceeded from Him in terms of affirming the truthfulness of Allah's Messengers or as an endowed honour to some of His chosen servants.

The Second: Is Hidden Grace (*al-Lutf al-Khafī*), which operates through unseen control over things from within. This involves directing mental and psychological processes in a specific direction, unnoticed by humans, to achieve a desired outcome. An example of this is found in the Quran's account[47] of the inspiration given to the mother of Mūsā when she was unsure what to do with her infant, fearing that Pharaoh might kill him. Allah placed in her heart the assurance and guidance needed to save him.

Thus, the instinct to seek refuge in a higher being capable of aiding humans in times of weakness and need is deeply ingrained in human nature, as evidenced by the course of human life.

---

47. See: *Sūrat al-Qaṣaṣ*: 7.

If the Creator is the one who planted this innate tendency within humanity, then He has also provided a corresponding response to it. Just as He placed in an infant the instinct to seek its mother for sustenance and care, He placed in the mother the instinct to respond to her child with love and compassion.

This manifestation is highlighted in several Quranic verses. Allah says: {*Allah is Graceful with His servants; He sustains whom He wills. And He is the Powerful, the Mighty*}.[48] And He said: {*Who is it that responds to the desperate one when he calls upon Him and removes evil?*}[49] And He said: {*And when My servants ask you concerning Me—indeed I am near. I respond to the call of the supplicant when he calls upon Me. So let them respond to Me and believe in Me that they may be rightly guided*}.[50] And He said: {*And when they board a ship, they supplicate Allah, in sincere devotion to Him. But when He delivers them to the land, at once they associate others with Him*}.[51] And He said: {*And when you are afflicted with adversity at sea, those you worship besides Him desert you. But when He delivers you to the land, you turn away [from Him]. And man is ever ungrateful*}.[52]

---

48. See: *Sūrat al-Shūrā*: 19.
49. See: *Sūrat al-Naml*: 62.
50. See: *Sūrat al-Baqara*: 186.
51. See: *Sūrat al-ʿAnkabūt*: 65.
52. See: *Sūrat al-Isrāʾ*: 67.

However, this form of divine response does not occur in such a way, either quantitatively or qualitatively, where it disrupts the natural laws and decrees governing life. The inherent structure of life, including death, the decay of things, and the occurrence of illnesses and causes, remains intact. Allah responds to His servants in ways they do not anticipate, without contradicting the system of life, except in cases where an explicit intervention through miracles and extraordinary events is necessitated.

This principle applies universally, even to the Prophets and the righteous. Divine response to their prayers is not unconditional, nor is assistance given to them without limits.

Creator's Love and Affection

The Fifth Manifestation: Is that the relationship between the Creator and humanity is one of love and affection. Allah loves humanity's knowledge of Him, their connection with Him, and their appreciation of His blessings. Numerous verses affirm His attributes (Glorified is He) toward humanity as mercy, kindness, compassion, patience, and love—not only for the believers but for humanity at large. He is more compassionate toward His servants than a mother toward her child, as stated in the hadith.

Humans have been created with the capacity to know Allah, to communicate with Him, and to learn from Him. They have been endowed with intellect, which is the tool of understanding, contemplation, learning, and teaching, as well as communication and expression. This innate curiosity and drive to explore the mysteries of the universe and existence have been implanted within them.

Similarly, Allah has instilled within humans a conscience, which forms the foundation of ethics, which beyond organising human interactions, prepares individuals to feel gratitude toward their Creator and to uphold courtesy in their relationship with Him.

Moreover, He has subjected the possibilities of the universe to their benefit, promised assistance when they turn to Him, and sent Messengers to clarify the realities and horizons of life.

So He (Glorified is He), desires that humans recognise Him and His blessings, live in a state of gratitude and appreciation, and maintain a relationship with Him marked by the propriety of connection and respect. Belief, therefore, is considered an act of gratitude toward Allah. He says: {*If you disbelieve— indeed, Allah is free from need of you. Nor does He approve of disbelief for His servants. If you are grateful, He is pleased [to see] it in you*}.[53] And He says: {*Indeed, We guided him to the way, be he grateful or ungrateful*}.[54] And He says: {*And I did not create the jinn and mankind except to worship Me*}.[55]

---

53. See: *Sūrat al-Zumar*: 7.
54. See: *Sūrat al-Insān*: 3.
55. See: *Sūrat al-Dhāriyāt*: 56.

In numerous verses, after mentioning the blessings He has bestowed upon humanity and the creatures He has subjected to their service, Allah states: {*So that you may give thanks*}.[56] Allah also reproaches humanity for failing to fulfill the duty of gratitude owed to Him. After listing His blessings, He declares: {*It is Allah who created the heavens and the earth and sent down rain from the sky and produced thereby some fruits as sustenance for you and subjected the ships for you to sail through the sea by His command; and He also subjected the rivers for you. * He also subjected the sun and the moon for you, continuous [in orbit], and subjected the night and the day for you. * And He gave you from all you asked of Him. And should you count the favours of Allah, you could not enumerate them. Indeed, mankind is unjust and ungrateful*}.[57]

Granting Serenity to Humanity

The Sixth Manifestation[58]: Is that the Creator of the universe (Glorified is He), is the Lord of all His creations, nurturing each according to its nature. For humanity, equipped with intellect and conscience, His Lordship involves a unique form of care. This is unlike the nurturing of plants or animals, but rather a special nurturing that can be likened—though Allah's example is far greater—to the nurturing of parents

---

56. See: *Sūrat al-Anfāl*: 26; *al-Naḥl*: 41, 78; *al-Ḥajj*: 36; *al-Qaṣaṣ*: 73; *al-Jāthiya*: 12.
57. See: *Sūrat Ibrāhīm*: 32-34.
58. This stems from the aforementioned manifestation (i.e. The Fifth Manifestation).

for their children, as opposed to the care animals provide their offspring.[59]

Among the aspects of this special relationship between Allah the Exalted and His creation—beyond His assistance and attention—is the sense of inner tranquility and peace that He instills in humans, a fundamental human need.

This divine tranquility resembles the security provided by states and companies through insurance, which gives individuals peace of mind during times of need in exchange for monetary contributions. It also resembles the psychological comfort children derive from the presence of their parents. For example, if a child is aware of their father's existence, even if the father has passed away, the family might not inform the child immediately, saying instead that he is travelling. This preserves the child's sense of psychological security and prevents feelings of emptiness or distress.

Life as a Test for Humanity

However, one must note that Allah (Glorified is He), despite extending special care to humanity, showing love and affection for them, He endowed humanity with free-will,

---

59. It is for this reason that some scriptures of the divine religions have described Allah (Blessed and Exalted is He) as "Our Father, Who art in heaven." If this expression is to be deemed correct, then its origin lies in the divine care Allah extends to His creation.

allowing individuals to make their choices and chart their paths. His wisdom has determined that human life is to serve as a racetrack. Thus, people compete in this arena, each being granted the outcome of what they pursue. Their ranks differ according to their efforts and their levels of commitment; and so the virtuous and the wicked, the complete and the deficient, are not equal.

So if a person devotes themselves to fulfilling what Allah desires, recognising Him, showing gratitude, honouring His blessings, and accepting His message, Allah increases His care for them, grants them more blessings, and bestows upon them special guardianship. As He (the Mighty) says: {*If you are grateful, I will give you more*}.[60]

However, if a person neglects this out of ingratitude and denial, they are considered rebellious toward Allah and are left to their own devices, stripped of the blessings of divine care.

If ignorance is the cause of neglect—even with a valid excuse—it remains a deficiency that prevents the individual from attaining the rank of one who is knowledgeable and grateful to Allah. However, it does not lower them to the level of one who is ungrateful and denies His blessings. The ignorant person is neither equal to the ungrateful denier nor to the knowledgeable and thankful servant.

---

60. See: *Sūrat Ibrāhīm*: 7.

Creator's Message to Humanity

The Seventh Manifestation: Is that Allah (the Exalted) sent a message to them—through individuals chosen from among His creation—to remind them of all the previously mentioned foundational truths. This message aims to provide clarity about the system of existence, the nature of life, and humanity's role within it. It also offers legislative guidance by calling humanity to align with the principles of innate human disposition, such as respecting rights and pursuing virtues. Moreover, it draws attention to life as a competitive arena where every action, whether good or evil, crystallises in accordance to their value in another realm. Allah says: {*He who created death and life to test you [as to] which of you is best in deed*}.[61] And He said: {*Each community has its own direction to which it turns. So race toward good deeds*}.[62]

Commitment to Guardianship (*Wilāya*)

The Eighth Manifestation: Is that while the Creator nurtures all His servants universally through the laws He has established in the cosmos and creation, He has committed to a special guardianship (*wilāya*) for those among His creation who believe in Him. Those who place their faith in Allah, rely on Him, maintain good thoughts about Him, and entrust their affairs to Him are granted His guardianship in proportion to

---

61. See: *Sūrat al-Mulk*: 2.
62. See: *Sūrat al-Baqara*: 148.

their willingness to accept it and their regard for what He has conveyed to them.

However, He (Glorified is He) does not compel them to accept this guardianship, for life is built upon the principle of human free-will. As He says: {*Could we force you to accept it against your will?*}[63] And He says: {*There shall be no compulsion in [acceptance of] the religion. The right course has become clear from the wrong*}.[64]

The relationship between humanity and Allah in this regard—though Allah's example is far greater—resembles that of a child to a wise and caring father. To the extent that the child loves, obeys, and submits to the father's guardianship, the father—whether consciously perceived by the child or not—guides them toward wisdom and happiness. Conversely, if the child turns away, resists, and rejects the father's involvement, the father leaves them to manage their own affairs.

This concept is highlighted in multiple verses of the Quran. Allah says: {*We are your protectors in this worldly life and in the Hereafter*}.[65] And He says: {*Allah is the guardian of those who believe; He brings them out from darknesses into the light.*}[66]

---

63. See: *Sūrat Hūd*: 28.
64. See: *Sūrat al-Baqara*: 257.
65. See: *Sūrat Fuṣṣilat*: 31.
66. See: *Sūrat al-Baqara*: 257.

And He said: {*And Allah is the guardian of the believers*}.[67] And the Exalted also said: {*And Allah is the protector of the righteous*}.[68] These verses notify one of the emphasis that Allah's guardianship strengthens in accordance with an individual's belief and by their reaching the rank of piety (*taqwā*). Whoever believes in Allah without rejecting Him or denying His Messengers is granted His guardianship in proportion to their reliance on Him, their understanding of Him, and their appreciation of what has been conveyed to them about Him.

Two Divine Systems: Existential (*Takwīnī*) and Legislative (*Tashrī'ī*)

The Ninth Manifestation: Is evident in the dual systems He has established in His creation:

One of them: Is the existential system, which governs all beings, including the human being; it was established in a specific manner, and is characterised by the design and natural laws that Allah has ordained for all creatures, ensuring harmony and consistency in accordance with His attribute of Wisdom (Blessed and Exalted is He).

---

67. See: *Sūrat Āl 'Imrān*: 68.
68. See: *Sūrat al-Jāthiya*: 19.

This divine will, which necessitates the operation of this system, is referred to as "Existential Will (*al-Irāda al-Takwīniyya*)".

While this system applies universally to the cosmos and all its beings, it encompasses within each creature a unique structure tailored to its nature.

For instance, humans, distinguished by their intellect, reasoning, moral conscience, and free-will, are governed by laws and systems appropriate to their nature. This is evident in the legislative system that guides their actions and responsibilities.

Additionally, within the natural laws governing creation, there are provisions for the Creator's special relationship with humanity, including His care and responsiveness, as previously described.

The Second of Them: Is the legislative system, which is designed to regulate the actions of rational beings with free-will, directing them toward the correct and beneficial path for themselves and their species—aligned with the overarching existential system.

This divine will, which necessitates the legislative system, is referred to as "Legislative Will (*al-Irāda al-Tashrīʿiyya*)", representing another aspect of Allah's care for humanity.

Naturally, Allah's existential will does not coerce rational beings into compliance with the legislative system, as doing so would negate their free-will and render the system part of the existential order rather than a framework of moral and ethical choices.

As a result, the existential laws governing creation are subject to human utilisation, by His permission, allowing individuals to exercise their free-will within this framework. Consequently, humans may misuse tools and systems created under existential laws to commit injustice or oppression against others. Such misuse produces its natural effects unless the oppressed turn to Allah for aid, prompting divine intervention in accordance with specific laws of intervention, as previously explained. This allowance for natural processes to unfold does not imply that Allah's permission (Glorified is He) for such actions entails any injustice on His part toward His servants.

Thus, it becomes clear:

1. It is erroneous for a person to attribute the consequences of their choices to Allah, framing them as predestined and inevitable, thereby absolving themselves of responsibility. Such an act is akin to fabricating lies against Allah concerning creation, a sin and transgression no less severe than inventing lies about His legislation.

By extension: It is equally wrong to attribute negative societal outcomes and erroneous phenomena to Allah as inevitably predetermined. Such claims can lead to a complacency within society, deterring efforts for reform and exacerbating problems. Allah says: {*And if only the people of the cities had believed and feared Allah, We would have bestowed blessings upon them from the heavens and the earth; but they belied [the truth], so We seized them for their misdeeds*}.[69]

2. It is also incorrect for a person to justify their actions by claiming that Allah (the Exalted) permitted them, as He says: {*And they said, 'If the Most Merciful had willed, we would not have worshipped them.' They have no knowledge of that; they do nothing but lie*}.[70] Likewise, it is flawed to argue that refraining from an action is justified because Allah has not permitted it with regards to them, as illustrated in His statement: {*And when it is said to them, 'Spend from what Allah has provided for you,' those who disbelieve say to those who believe, 'Why should we feed those that Allah could have fed if He willed? You are not but in clear error!'*}[71]

3. That Allah's permission for a person to act according to their free-will, even if their actions are wrongful or

---

69. See: *Sūrat al-Aʿrāf*: 96.
70. See: *Sūrat al-Zukhruf*: 20.
71. See: *Sūrat Yā-Sīn*: 47.

sinful, does not negate His disapproval of such actions in a legislative sense. This disapproval is expressed through prohibitions and warnings against actions that are harmful to humanity. This balance arises from divine wisdom in establishing and maintaining natural laws within the human environment, while preserving human free-will.

This concept can be likened—though Allah's example is far greater—to the actions of a father who organises the household by providing tools, resources, and facilities. However, he might prohibit his child from using a particular tool at a specific time or for certain purposes out of concern for their well-being. Despite having the ability to prevent the child from using it altogether, the father refrains from doing so. Instead, he allows the child to exercise their free-will and not let them imitate his own personal preference, while allowing them to bear the responsibility for their actions, thus learning from their choices. This is while he simultaneously doesn't see a greater benefit in intervening and preventing the child on the basis of his desires.

Compensation for Human Suffering

The Tenth Manifestation[72]: Are the aspects of the suffering they endure in this life, which they are afflicted with involuntarily and are unable to prevent. This is such as

---

72. Which is connected to what has just been mentioned.

injustices inflicted by others, illness, or unavoidable poverty. These forms of suffering have three dimensions according to religious texts:

The First of Them: Is that such suffering arises from the natural laws and universal order upon which creation and life are built. The preservation and consistency of this order necessitate these occurrences.

In the Islamic texts these are referred to as "decrees (*maqādīr*)" that cannot be avoided or altered.

The Second: Is that suffering serves as part of an individual's test. If a person endures these trials with patience and seeks divine reward without transgressing the boundaries of virtue, they achieve a level of distinction that is unattainable for those who do not face such trials. The Quran frequently describes hardships and adversities as a means of testing the people.

The Third: Is that every instance of suffering endured involuntarily—according to the signification of the religious texts—is recorded as a merit in the individual's account with Allah (Blessed and Exalted is He). They are rewarded for it or have their sins diminished as a result. Every deprivation or hardship in this life comes with compensation and rectification in a manner determined by Allah (Glorified is He). Similarly, every blessing carries a responsibility, as the Quran states: {*On that day, you will be asked about your* *pleasures*}.⁷³ And in the words of Imam ʿAlī (peace be upon him): *"For what is lawful, there is accounting, and for what is unlawful, there is punishment."*⁷⁴

It is also incumbent to note that while Allah (Glorified is He) does no rationally abhorrent (*qabīḥ*) thing and commits no injustice, the principles of [rationally cognised] moral goodness (*ḥusn*) and moral evil (*qubḥ*) concerning Him—as the Creator of life—differ from those applied to humanity, who are created beings bound by a specific moral order. If a person has the ability to remove an injustice afflicting others and fails to act, their heart is sinful. However, this does not apply to Allah, who has established the universe on the basis of specific laws and systems. Allah is not obligated to intervene in every injustice, as such interventions would conflict with the established natural laws and their broader purposes. In fact, such disruptions could undermine the greater order and objectives of the system. He (the Exalted) said: {*And if it were not for Allah driving [some] people back by the means of others, the earth would have been corrupted; but Allah is bountiful to the worlds*}.⁷⁵

---

73. See: *Sūrat al-Takāthur*: 8.
74. See: *Nahj al-Balāgha*, pg. 106.
75. See: *Sūrat al-Baqara*: 251.

Error of Prescribing Things to Allah

It is also incumbent to note that adopting a presumptive approach toward Allah (Glorified is He)—where one makes demands or prescribes how He should act—this is misguided and does not lead to truth. When definite evidence confirms Allah's justice, wisdom, and benevolence, and the rightful nature of His deeds, this should serve as a foundation for understanding His actions. Any ambiguous or perplexing matters should be interpreted within the framework of this foundational understanding, and knowledge of their details should be entrusted to the Creator. This is consistent with the approach rational individuals adopt in other contexts; for example, when a person recognises sufficient signs of a doctor's expertise or a parent's wisdom, it is logical to refrain from constant questioning or proposals in matters that appear obscure.

The Quran highlights this principle when recounting the rejection of the proposals made by people to the Prophets. Allah says: {*And [recall] when you said, 'O Moses, we will never believe you until we see Allah manifestly.' At that, thunderbolts struck you as you looked on*}.[76] And He said: {*And when a sign comes to them, they say, 'We will never believe until we are given like that which was given to the Messengers of Allah.' Allah is most knowing of where He places His message*}.[77] And the

---

76. See: *Sūrat al-Baqara*: 55.
77. See: *Sūrat al-Anʿām*: 124.

Exalted said: {*And they say, 'We will not believe you until you cause a spring to gush forth for us from the earth, * or [until] you have a garden of palm trees and grapes and make rivers gush forth within them in forceful torrents, * or you make the heaven fall upon us in fragments as you have claimed, * or you bring Allah and the angels before [us], or you have a house of gold or you ascend into the sky. And [even then], we will not believe in your ascension until you bring down to us a book we may read.' Say, 'Exalted is my Lord! Was I ever but a human Messenger?'*}[78]

This concludes the discussion on the first aspect of the Creator's care for humanity.

Human Nature and Destiny

As for the second aspect—of the religious view of humanity—this concerns the essence of the human according to the religious perspective. This can be clarified through several matters.

Innate Awareness of the Divine

The First Matter: Is that humanity is innately predisposed to sense the existence of a transcendent being and to feel a need for such a presence, especially in moments of vulnerability and need. Spiritual well-being, in general, cannot be achieved

---

78. See: *Sūrat al-Isrā'*: 90-93.

without cognising this being, having a connection with Him, presenting one's needs to Him, and a conscious fear of His accountability. Psychological equilibrium is unattainable without belief in Him; otherwise, a person experiences feelings of emptiness and a void in their life. This feeling is akin to a child's instinctive need for their parents, which is only pacified through connection with them.

Perhaps, evidence for this sense in one's conscience can be found through an inductive study of the emotional and psychological states of those who do not adhere to religious beliefs, particularly during times of weakness and desperation, affirming the deeply ingrained nature of this awareness.

However, this sense may become obscured during times of luxury and ease, only to resurface in moments of hardship, fear, or awe at witnessing the wonders of creation. In some cases, it may be denied outright due to stubbornness against one's innate disposition or as an attempt to evade the responsibilities that come with acknowledgment and affirmation.

It is not problematic that this innate sense of a transcendent being requires stimulation to emerge and transition into conscious awareness. Many emotions and predispositions within humans require external prompts to activate them. This does not imply that such feelings are acquired from external factors, as is well-known amongst contemporary psychologists. Allah has said: {*And when they board a ship, they supplicate Allah, in sincere devotion to Him. But when He delivers them to the land, at once they associate others with Him*}.[79] And He (may He be Glorified) said: {*And when We bestow favour upon man, he turns away and distances himself; but when he is afflicted with evil, he turns to prolonged prayer*}.[80]

This idea is also suggested in other Quranic verses and transmitted traditions. Allah says: {*So direct your face toward the religion, inclining to truth. [Adhere to] the fiṭra (natural disposition) of Allah upon which He has created [all] people. No change should there be in the creation of Allah. That is the correct religion, but most of the people do not know*}.[81] Moreover, Allah states: {*And [mention] when your Lord took from the children of Adam—from their loins—their descendants and made them testify of themselves, [saying to them], 'Am I not your Lord?' They said, 'Indeed, we testify to this'*}.[82] And the Prophet Muḥammad (peace be upon him and his progeny) said: "*Every child is born upon the fiṭra (natural disposition).*"[83] And it has already been mentioned that Imam ʿAlī (peace be upon him) said: "*He sent to them His Prophets in succession to*

---

79. See: *Sūrat al-ʿAnkabūt*: 65.
80. See: *Sūrat Fuṣṣilat*: 51.
81. See: *Sūrat al-Rūm*: 30. The meaning is derived from the context of the preceding verses, which critique polytheism and affirm that monotheism aligns with humanity's natural disposition (*fiṭra*).
82. See: *Sūrat al-Aʿrāf*: 172.
83. *al-Kāfī*, Vol. 2, pg. 13; *Musnad Aḥmad*, Vol. 2, pg. 233 and other sources.

fulfil the pledges of His creation, to remind them of His forgotten favours, to establish the truth by conveying His message, to revive their numbed intellects. He instructed [his Prophets] to show them the signs of His power: the roof of the sky above them raised high, the cradle of the earth beneath them spread wide, the means of livelihood that give them life, the appointed times of death that bring an end to them, the ailments that wear them out, and the successive events that befall them."[84]

Therefore, this innate sense, embedded within human predisposition, serves as a reinforcement for what the intellect cognises about the existence of a Creator who governs the universe and grants life. Through contemplation of the intricate beauty and precision of creation, this awareness naturally aligns with submission to the unseen and belief in Allah. Perhaps this is the secret behind the human being's complete harmony and resonance with acknowledging the unseen and affirming faith in Allah.

Life Beyond Death

The Second Matter: Pertains to the human entity, which is not merely a physical body that perishes with death. Rather, the human is a composite of body and soul. The soul persists after death, while the body will be reconstituted at the appointed time of resurrection, at which point the individual will be recompensed for their deeds, whether good or evil.

---

84. *Nahj al-Balāgha*, pg. 43, Sermon 1.

This notion perhaps finds resonance in human emotions, as individuals are often preoccupied with their destiny after death, as though their very being is inclined toward enduring existence. Even those who are not religious regard the deceased—particularly figures of greatness or intellectual distinction—as having a form of continued presence in another realm, wishing them well, happiness, and peace.

It is conceivable that this intrinsic feeling is intertwined with the truth of humanity's enduring nature after death, serving as an indicator of this reality. This connection may reflect the broader harmony between human emotions and the reality of human existence and purpose in life.

Divine Guidance for Humanity

The Third Matter: Is that the human being has been endowed with further guidance to navigate toward their best interests in this life. They have been equipped with numerous capacities and potentials, as will be elaborated upon.

1. (**The Intellect**): The faculty through which humans cognise things, serving as the foundation for all human capacities. Allah (Glorified is He) said: {*Say, it is He who brought you into being and made for you hearing, vision, and hearts [for understanding]; little are you grateful*}.[85]

---

85. See: *Sūrat al-Mulk*: 23.

2. (**The Conscience**): The innate sense by which humans discern what ought to be done, embodying the spirit of virtue within. Allah (Glorified is He) said: {*And by the soul and how He proportioned it, ∗ and inspired it with discernment of its wickedness and its righteousness. ∗ He has succeeded who purifies it, ∗ and the one instills it [with corruption] has failed*}.[86]

3. (**The Spirit of Wisdom**): The faculty that enables a person to evaluate harm and benefit, considering both immediate and long-term outcomes, so they may choose what is most advantageous. This is reflected in the example struck in the Exalted's words: {*Have they not travelled through the land with hearts to understand?*}[87] Here, travelling through the land stimulates the spirit of wisdom and reflection within the human being.

4. (**Natural Desires**): Inclinations that ensure the preservation of the individual and the species, such as the desire for status, wealth, food, parenthood, and marriage.

These desires are, in themselves, unlimited and not inherently confined by the bounds of wisdom or virtue. They are psychological tendencies that drive a person to seek their fulfillment. However, it is the individual's

---

86. See: *Sūrat al-Shams*: 7-10.
87. See: *Sūrat al-Ḥajj*: 46.

duty to refrain from indulging these desires beyond their proper limits, for doing so would turn them into afflictions that harm the individual's life, akin to other diseases.

5. (**Freedom of Choice**): The steering faculty of human life, enabling a person to direct their actions either toward intellection, wisdom, and conscience, or toward unchecked actions that drive towards an overindulgence in desires, as has been mentioned in the glorious verse: *{Indeed, We guided him to the way, whether he be grateful or ungrateful}*.[88]

The guidance that a person ought to follow in life—to achieve their interests and ward off harm—lies in cognising matters through the intellect, followed by striving freely while inspired by the spirits of wisdom and virtue.

This is the religion's analysis of human nature and their psychological faculties. Certain atheistic or deistic perspectives, however, do not recognise this hierarchy of human attributes or the guidance structured around humanity's reality. Instead, they assert that human beings lack free-will and are involuntarily driven in their actions by hereditary and environmental factors.

---

88. See: *Sūrat al-Insān*: 3.

These perspectives also reject the existence of innate moral values within humans. They claim that human behavior is governed solely by the logic of weakness and strength: any emotion labeled as "moral" is merely an expression of weakness, while any emotion deemed "immoral" is an expression of strength.

This viewpoint finds support in the theory of evolution, which posits that humans evolved from animals whose behavior is driven purely by instinct. These instincts dominate animals, and humans, according to this theory, are no different except for their ability to think, which enables them to devise more complex ways to fulfill their instincts and desires.

Legislation, in accordance to this perspective, does not represent elevated values—even within democratic systems. Instead, it is merely a tool for organising social life according to collective interests when a group is able to impose its will through the majority.

Ethical and Mechanistic Laws

The Fourth Matter: Is that human life is arranged according to laws that lead to different outcomes, whether good or evil. Some of these laws are ethical and some are mechanistic.

The ethical laws pertain to virtues and vices. Virtues are the laws of goodness and prosperity, both in this life and beyond. Every virtuous trait is a sign of happiness, and every virtuous action heralds well-being. Conversely, vices are the laws of harm and misery in life; every vile trait is a marker of suffering, and every base action portends misfortune and hardship. Thus, it is incumbent upon individuals to be mindful of these laws and their consequences when making choices in their lives.

The mechanistic laws[89], on the other hand, are laws that yield different outcomes depending on how they are employed. If utilised for good, they produce positive results; if exploited for harm, they yield negative consequences. The influence and outcomes of these laws and principles are evident to people, who continually harness them to achieve their goals.

For instance, natural laws and principles can be employed to benefit humanity and meet its needs, just as they can be misused for oppression and aggression. This is exemplified by nuclear physics, which can be utilised to treat a number of terminal illnesses and generate electrical power, but also exploited to produce nuclear weapons with devastating effects on humans and the environment.

Among these mechanistic laws: Is the principle that collective social changes inevitably bring about corresponding

---

89. The term "mechanistic" is used here to indicate that these laws function as tools for objectives—whether good or evil—depending on their applications and purposes.

effects. If there is no collective change within a society, its conditions and circumstances will not improve.

This universal principle can be harnessed to reform and advance society by steering change toward betterment. Conversely, if societal change heads toward deterioration, the result will inevitably be societal corruption and instability, as highlighted in the verse: {*Indeed, Allah does not change the condition of a people until they change what is in themselves*}.[90]

Creator's Non-Neglect of Humanity

The Fifth Matter: Building upon what has been previously discussed, Allah, the Exalted, has not abandoned humanity in this life. Rather, He has established for them a clear path and a defined law conveyed through intermediaries—who are His Prophets. Adherence to this path has been made the guarantor of human happiness in both this life and the next. Conversely, deviation from it has been decreed as the cause of human misery. Whoever follows and adheres to this divine path will be under Allah's care and will be rewarded. He will bless their life and grant them enduring happiness. On the other hand, those who forsake it are left to their own devices, entrusted to themselves to bear the consequences of their misdeeds.

---

90. See: *Sūrat al-Ra'd*: 11.

Thus, the degrees of human happiness or misery in the afterlife vary in accordance with their adherence to this divine law. Those whose actions are virtuous and upright will reap abundant good in the hereafter, whereas those whose deeds are vile and corrupt in this life will face misery in the eternal abode.

Religious Anthropology

Religious Legislation

As for the fourth perspective: One of the aspects of the religious view of the universe and life is the legislative perspective of religion, which includes the clarification of the foundations of religious law that align with the religious worldview concerning the Creator, the universe, and humanity, as detailed earlier. This perspective can be summarised in the following matters...

Alignment of Law with Human Nature

The First Matter: The best legislation for human life is that which aligns with both their material and psychological makeup. Any other form of legislation—though it may initially appear beneficial and enticing to society for a period—ultimately leads to negative reactions and unintended consequences. These effects gradually accumulate over time, eventually causing the system to be rejected or can turn it into a dilemma for the individual or society.

Innate Basis of Religious Law

The Second Matter: The appropriate legislation for human creation is inherent within their natural disposition. As Allah, the Exalted said: {*And [He] inspired it [the soul] with discernment of its wickedness and its righteousness.*}.[91] And He also said: {*But Allah has endeared the faith to you and has made it beautiful to your hearts; and He has made hateful to you disbelief, wickedness, and disobedience. Those are the rightly guided*}.[92]

Depth of Religious and Human Laws

The Third Matter: Legislation from the religious perspective is profoundly deeper than human statutory legislation Human legislation resembles an instrument of coercion and obligation, laying the groundwork for punitive rulings. The penalties associated with its violation are primarily deterrent in nature, aiming at social reform and, at times, individual reform as well.

In contrast, religious legislation perceives virtuous and wise actions, as well as their opposites, as integral to the eternal structure of the human being. They become foundational elements of their lasting essence, shaping their growth and contributing to their existential composition. As Allah (the Exalted) says: {*Say, 'Everyone acts according to their own way,*

---

91. See: *Sūrat al-Shams*: 8.
92. See: *Sūrat al-Ḥujurāt*: 7.

but your Lord is most knowing of who follows the best-guided path.'}[93] This applies regardless of whether others are aware of the action, praise it, or reward it. Allah also says: {*On the Day when their tongues, their hands, and their feet will bear witness against them regarding they used to do*}[94] and: {*Indeed, the hearing, the sight, and the heart—all those will be questioned*}.[95]

Thus, this life is a preparatory stage for humanity. If a person is cultivated in it with righteous guidance, they develop a sound heart and a purified soul, earning their appropriate rank and reward in the Hereafter. As Allah says: {*Except he who comes to Allah with a sound heart*}.[96] On the other hand, if one is raised poorly, resulting in a sinful heart[97], they will receive the consequences of their actions in the afterlife.

This worldly life, with its joys and hardships, its pleasures and sorrows, serves as a training ground. Each person can transform it into a pathway for either virtuous development or moral corruption.

---

93. See: *Sūrat al-Isrāʾ*: 84.
94. See: *Sūrat al-Nūr*: 24.
95. See: *Sūrat al-Isrāʾ*: 36.
96. See: *Sūrat al-Shuʿarāʾ*: 89.
97. As Allah has said with regards to the one who conceals their testimony: {*And do not conceal testimony, for whoever conceals it—his heart is indeed sinful*}, See: *Sūrat al-Baqara*: 283.

Religious Law and Innate Rights

The Fourth Matter: The foundation of religious legislation lies in the observance of innate rights, divided into primary and secondary categories.

Thus, the primary innate rights are:

1. The right of Allah, the Exalted, who is the Creator, Sustainer, and Bestower of blessings upon humanity. This right requires the observance of etiquette as defined in religious practices, including specific acts of worship such as prayer, fasting, pilgrimage, *i'tikāf*[98], expiation, repentance, and seeking forgiveness. It also includes the general remembrance of Allah through praise, gratitude, and compliance.

2. The right of parents, who are the origin of a person's existence and who provide care and upbringing. This right prohibits attributing oneself to others through adoption and mandates dealing with one's parents with kindness, especially in their old age.

3. The right of kinship, which arises from the natural bond between family members. This connection is a fundamental aspect of human nature, making it

---

98. [Translator's note:] This refers to a form of worship where one stays at a mosque for a period of at least three days and fasts. Its specific conditions and boundaries have been discussed in the works of jurisprudence.

obligatory to maintain family ties and prohibiting their severance.

4. The right of neighbours, as physical proximity has a profound impact on human nature. This right becomes particularly significant in cases of long-term closeness, which can evoke natural concerns and obligations toward one's neighbors.

5. The right of religious brotherhood among those who share the same faith, as this bond represents spiritual closeness and a shared culture that guides a person towards the correct path. This relationship should be free from fanaticism and injustice toward others who do not share the same belief.

6. The right of human brotherhood, which is a common connection among all people. This right obliges individuals to treat each other with respect and fairness according to the law of nature, even when there is a difference in faith. Allah says: {*Allah does not forbid you from dealing kindly and justly to those who do not fight you because of religion and do not expel you from your homes. Indeed, Allah loves those who are just*}.[99] In the words of Imam ʿAlī (peace be upon him): *"People are of two*

---

99. See: *Sūrat al-Mumtaḥana*: 8.

> *types: either your brother in religion, or your counterpart in creation."*[100]

7. The right of animals, which involves not harming them without a rational justification. It is also necessary to care for and maintain animals if they are owned, and it is forbidden to kill them cruelly. The Holy Book forbids eating animals that are strangled (*al-mukhannaqa*),[101] beaten to death, or killed by another animal.[102] The Prophet's teachings also emphasise the humane slaughter of animals with a sharp instrument, as the wisdom behind this is to avoid unnecessary suffering for the animal. Additionally, it is forbidden to confine animals without care or a rational purpose.[103]

8. The right of the self to respond to its natural desires without excess or waste. This includes the inherent desire for life, which is why the law forbids taking

---

100. See: *Nahj al-Balāgha*, pg. 70.
101. "The strangled" refers to an animal that dies from suffocation, "the beaten" refers to one that is struck with a stick or similar object until it dies, and "the gored" refers to an animal killed by being gored by another animal like it.
102. See: *Sūrat al-Māʾida*: 3.
103. There are other pieces of advice in the religion regarding water and the environment, which one finds to be of wisdom, good taste, and aims to organise life. This can be found in things such as the prohibition of cutting down trees in war, and the prohibition of urinating in water, and other such things.

one's own life. It also includes the desire for safety, which prohibits causing significant harm to oneself. Additionally, the desire for health is emphasised, with numerous health-related teachings found in the books of hadith, particularly regarding food and drink, advising the individual to maintain their health.

As for the secondary natural rights, these are rights that arise from obligations, such as promises, covenants, and trusts—even with enemies. Allah says: {*Indeed, Allah commands you to return things entrusted to you to their rightful owners*}.[104] He also says: {*Fulfill the contracts*}.[105] Regarding agreements with non-Muslims, He says: {*If they are upright with you, be upright with them*}.[106; 107]

---

104. See: *Sūrat al-Nisāʾ*: 58.
105. See: *Sūrat al-Māʾida*: 1.
106. See: *Sūrat al-Tawba*: 7.
107. These rights, particularly in their specific details, distinguish religious teachings from certain modern cultures. For instance, the rights of parents and their satisfaction with their children is often neglected in Western culture, leading to an increasing phenomenon of children abandoning their elderly parents in care homes. While children are naturally inclined to uphold this right, the prevailing culture does not prioritise it. Similarly, the right of neighbours to receive assistance and kindness is also overlooked in some societies, with neighbours often unaware of each other's circumstances or uninterested in helping. Some individuals, upon learning about Islamic culture, have expressed an interest in converting due to its natural approach to such rights, which fosters a sense of happiness without any materialistic motives or ulterior

Legislation and Noble Traits

The Fifth Matter: This legislation takes into account human noble traits, obliging their adoption in certain areas, and recommending their adoption in others, based on the level of rational goodness and abhorrence in each case, as well as the positive and negative consequences resulting from them. Religious legislation does not only call for the pursuit of virtues but emphasises the necessity of adhering to them, as they have profound effects on both the individual and society.

Among the human virtues that are frequently mentioned in the Quran and Sunna are:

1. Avoiding harm to others in terms of life, body, honour, reputation, or wealth, even in actions like mocking, backbiting, or abusing one's rights.

2. Kindness, especially towards those who have blessed us, such as parents, and those in need, such as the poor, orphans, and others.

3. Fulfilling obligations and keeping promises.

4. Chastity in responding to natural instincts in all its forms.

5. Gratitude for kindness and recognition of good deeds.

---

goals.

6. Modesty in keeping personal matters private and avoiding indecent speech.

7. Truthfulness, especially when giving testimony.

8. Politeness and respect, such as initiating greetings with peace.

9. Justice between people and impartiality with oneself.

10. Determination when it comes to reform and administering justice.

The encompassing terms for these virtuous traits and their opposites are *al-Ma'rūf* (the Known/the Good) and *al-Munkar* (the Unknown/the Evil). *al-Ma'rūf* refers to everything that is naturally recognised and accepted by the human conscience, while *al-Munkar* is everything that instinctively repels or is found objectionable.

Encouragement of *al-Ma'rūf* and prohibition of *al-Munkar* appear in many places in the Quran, and the command to promote the good and forbid the evil is even considered one of the signs of the truthfulness of the Prophet's mission (peace be upon him and his progeny).

Legal Rulings and *al-Ma'rūf* and *al-Munkar*

The basis of all rulings is to uphold the ten aforementioned virtues; they are a detailed and expanded explanation of these virtues and specific instances of their concepts…

Acts of worship, such as prayer and its related rituals, are etiquettes with Allah (Glorified is He), safeguarding His great right over people and His beneficence toward them. *Zakāt* (alms) is an act of kindness to the poor and a protection of general human welfare. Encouraging *al-ma'rūf* and discouraging *al-munkar* are acts of kindness both for the individuals directly addressed and for the broader community, as they are cooperative efforts toward righteousness and virtue. Contracts and agreements are commitments that must be honoured unless they lead to coercion or impose *al-munkar* and prohibitions. The obligation to cover faults, prevent temptation, and forbid marriage to close relatives protects chastity. Inheritance is an act of kindness to relatives and spouses, safeguarding the bond between them. The judiciary ensures justice and prevents oppression. Testimonies are tools for fair judgment. Penal rulings, such as *qiṣāṣ* (retaliation), *ḥudūd* (punishments), and *ta'zīr* (disciplinary measures), implement firmness and deter prohibited acts and evils, while *diyyāt* (blood money) compensates for wrongdoings.

Clear vs. Ambiguous Rights in Sharīʿa

The Sixth Matter: The rights and interests that a person observes are divided into two areas:

The First: A clear area, which the mind grasps explicitly and obviously. In this space, human nature, without confusion, dictates the rights, and religious legislation aligns with what human nature demands, as it is the Creator's law instilled within the human soul.

The Second: Grey areas, where the matter is unclear, and the mind cannot decisively conclude a clear position.[108] In these

---

108. There are two main reasons for the creation of these ambiguous areas:
    [1] The boundaries of certain concepts are not clearly distinguished from others, which requires legal intervention to clarify them. For example, the boundaries between countries, provinces, cities, or regions are often vague and require laws to define them clearly. Similarly, some general concepts, like "neighbourliness," have a clear area when a person's house is near another, but the boundaries become vague as the distance increases, leading to uncertainty about whether a home is considered a neighbor. Based on this, the core rights and entitlements are clear at the center but ambiguous at their periphery. For instance, if a person acquires land that satisfies their basic needs, they are naturally entitled to it by human nature. However, if they acquire vast expanses of land without needing some of it, the general nature becomes uncertain as to whether they are entitled to all of it compared to others who may need that unused land. Similarly, human nature judges that a child is not of legal maturity and

cases, it is necessary to defer to *Sharīʿa* in order to identify what wisdom and virtue dictate in these situations.

Wisdom in Ambiguous Areas

Islamic legislation addresses the ambiguous areas that challenge human intellect with rulings that reflect wisdom, virtue, and the general well-being of humanity. The religious texts provide guidance for managing the concerns these rulings may evoke, employing a persuasive and gentle approach, free from coercion or excessive imposition.

Examples of legislation whose wisdom has been clarified include:

1. **The Guardianship of Men Over Women:** This is explained in the noble verse: {*Men are the protectors and maintainers of women because of [the bounties] Allah has given to some more than others, and since they spend of their wealth*},[109] and the reasoning behind this ruling is

---

does not have the same rights as an adult, but as the child matures, there is uncertainty as to whether they have reached the age of maturity. In such cases, the law must decide.

[2] Human emotions such as excessive tenderness, harshness, or selfishness may lead to confusion about what constitutes noble or virtuous feelings, thus creating ambiguity in the judgment of their nobility or virtue. In such situations, there arises a grey area in determining the appropriate natural law.

109. See: *Sūrat al-Nisāʾ*: 34.

that the differences between men and women in various aspects of life necessitate that men bear the responsibility for guardianship within the family. This arrangement benefits both men and women, provided it is executed with fairness, and women respond appropriately to this role.

2. **The Differences in Rights and Entitlements Between Men and Women:** The reasoning for this is mentioned in the verse: {*Do not covet what Allah has given to some of you more than others, men have the portion they have earned; and women the portion they have earned. And ask Allah of His bounty. Indeed, Allah is ever, of all things, Knowing*}.[110] The different roles assigned to men and women—men being entrusted with defense, protection, and provision, and women with motherhood, house management, and nurturing—require different rulings for each gender.

3. **The Share of a Deceased Father in Inheritance Being Less Than That of His Children:** The father's share is limited to one-sixth, even when there is only one child, which may seem contrary to what would be expected in tribal societies where the father typically holds full control over the family's affairs, especially when the children are female or young. However, the noble verse addresses this, saying: {*Your fathers and your sons—you do not know which of them is more beneficial to you. This*

---

110. See: *Sūrat al-Nisā'*: 32.

is an obligation from Allah. Indeed, Allah is ever, of all things, Knowing and Wise}.[111] This statement implies that wealth is more appropriately passed on to the children, as they represent the future generation and are more beneficial in the long run. This arrangement aligns with human nature, as one's legacy should ideally continue through their offspring. The verse does not explicitly state that children are more beneficial than parents to avoid offending parents' feelings. Instead, it gently alludes to this truth, conveying that Allah's wisdom in favouring children in inheritance is not arbitrary or oppressive.

4. **The Prohibition of Alcohol Despite Its Deep Rootedness in Society:** The prohibition of alcohol, despite it being a difficult adjustment for the society to which the ruling was revealed, due to the fact they were addicted to its consumption, is explained in the verse: *{They ask you about wine and gambling. Say, 'In them is great harm and [yet some] benefit for people. But their harm is greater than their benefit.'}*[112] The prohibition serves as a gentle warning that, while alcohol may offer temporary relief from worries, the harm it causes—through impaired judgment, irresponsibility, and loss of awareness—far outweighs any potential benefit. This illustrates the wisdom behind the legislation: the harm of alcohol to

---

111. See: *Sūrat al-Nisā'*: 11.
112. See: *Sūrat al-Baqara*: 219.

the individual and society is far more detrimental than the fleeting pleasure it may provide.

5. **Legislation of *Qiṣāṣ* (Retribution):** The law of *qisas* is not justified based on a desire for arbitrary revenge or retaliation, as some might assume, especially since neither the slain individual nor their heirs benefit from the killing of the murderer. Rather, this ruling—though not inherently unjust to the killer (since it is a retributive measure in kind)—is in accordance with the public good. It serves as a deterrent; for anyone who knows that killing another will result in their own death will hesitate significantly before committing such an act. Allah says: {*Fair retribution saves life for you, people of understanding, so that you may guard yourselves against what is wrong*}.[113; 114]

6. **Not Granting Spoils of War (*Fay'*) to Combatants:** The decision to withhold the spoils of war (*fay'*)—which were not gained through direct military engagement, such as by cavalry or mounted troops—from the fighters, and

---

113. See: *Sūrat al-Baqara*: 179.
114. What has been said that statistics do not indicate the impact of killing on criminal deterrence is unclear; because accounting for the psychological motivations of the killer, according to the general rules of criminal behavior, requires that many potential murderers would be deterred by such a consequence. These statistics may be based on varying circumstances across the societies that were compared in these studies.

the refusal to yield to their greed for it, is explained in the verse: {*You [believers] did not have to spur on your horses or your camels for whatever gains Allah turned over to His Messenger from them. Allah gives authority to His Messengers over whom He wills, and Allah is capable of everything.* ✸ *As for the gains Allah has given to His Messenger from the people of the towns—it is for Allah, the Messenger, his kin, the orphans, the needy and the traveller, so that it will not be a perpetual distribution among the rich from you. And whatever the Messenger has given you—take it; and what he has prohibited for you—refrain from it. And fear Allah; indeed, Allah is severe in penalty*}.[115]

The meaning of this verse is that the combatants are not entitled to the *fay'* for two reasons:

One of them: Is their role in acquiring the *fay'* is not as active, as they did not gain it through cavalry or mounted troops.

The Other: If the *fay'* were to be distributed to the combatants, it would lead to corruption and harm to the general welfare, as it would become a wealth reserved only for the rich and the poor would be deprived.

7. **Prohibition of Attributing a Child to Someone Other than their Father Through Adoption,** which was a common practice in society at that time. The reasoning

---

115. See: *Sūrat al-Ḥashr*: 6-7.

provided in the religious texts is that legal paternity should align with biological paternity, as this best preserves the father's right to claim the child as his own. Allah says: {*He has not made your adopted sons your [real] sons. That is only your saying with your mouths. But Allah says the truth, and He guides to the way.* ∗ *Name your adopted sons after their real fathers; that is more just in the eyes of Allah. But if you do not know their fathers, then they are your brothers in religion and your close associates. And there is no blame upon you for what you made a mistake in, but only for what your hearts intended. And Allah is ever Forgiving and Merciful*}.[116]

8. **Prohibition of Likening One's Wife to One's Mother (*Ẓihār*),** a form of verbal declaration in pre-Islamic Arabia that would essentially suspend the wife's status as either a wife or a divorced woman. This practice was heavily criticised in the Quran. Allah says: {*Those who pronounce Ẓihār from among you [against their wives] are not their mothers. Their mothers are none but those who gave birth to them. And indeed, they are speaking an evil word and a lie. And indeed, Allah is Pardoning and Forgiving*}.[117]

9. **The Obligation of Fasting:** This was initially heavy on the Muslims. The Quran clarifies that the purpose of fasting is

---

116. See: *Sūrat al-Aḥzāb*: 4-5.
117. See: *Sūrat al-Mujādila*: 2.

to purify the soul and train the individual to control their desires. The fast is intended to increase one's awareness of Allah and the Hereafter, while detaching them from worldly distractions. Allah says: {*O you who have believed, fasting has been decreed upon you as it was decreed upon those before you that you may become pious*}.[118] Then, in the following verse, Allah adds: {*But if anyone does good of his own accord, it is better for him, and fasting is better for you, if only you knew*}.[119]

10. **The Obligation of Purification Before Prayer:** After it became clear that the ritual purification was burdensome to the people, the Quran reassures them that the purpose is not to cause hardship, but to purify them and complete Allah's blessings upon them. Allah says: {*Allah does not wish to place any burden on you: He only wishes to cleanse you and perfect His blessing on you, so that you may be thankful.*}.[120]

In these examples, we can observe that the divine texts provide an overall rationale for the wisdom behind these rulings, especially when addressing areas of ambiguity. The divine explanations aim to convince people by offering reasonable and coherent justifications, which align with wisdom and virtue. These justifications are based on sound,

---

118. See: *Sūrat al-Baqara*: 183.
119. See: *Sūrat al-Baqara*: 183.
120. See: *Sūrat al-Māʾida*: 6.

natural reasoning that appeals to the human instinct and understanding.

Two Pillars of Religious Law

The Seventh Matter: The religious legislative vision, in light of what has been discussed, relies—like the cosmic perspective—on two pillars: reasoning and devotion.

Reasoning applies in matters that are clearly understood by intellect, and not in immature, hasty forms of independent judgment, nor in arbitrary notions of what is considered "good" or "bad."

As for devotion and submission, it pertains to issues that lie in the ambiguous and unclear spaces where human intellect may struggle to form a clear judgment.

When reasoning is wrongly applied in matters of devotion, or when ritual submission is mistaken for reasoning—as done by the Khārijites and those who follow their example in contemporary times—a disruption occurs in religious education, and they stray from proper understanding and jurisprudence in the faith.

Example of Religious Education

The Eighth Matter: The example of religious education, which should be the ultimate goal for every religious person and a model for all believers of Allah—according to what is derived from the Quranic descriptions of believers and the qualities of the righteous—comprises two main elements.

One of them: Is the possession of all innate virtues, foremost among them gratitude to Allah, fulfilling His rights, justice, kindness, truthfulness, fulfilling trusts, altruism, and similar qualities.

The Other: Is the possession of rationality, embodied in mature judgment and sharp insight. For rationality is a fundamental aspect of the personality that religion seeks to nurture—contrary to the view of some people who initially see no connection between religion and reason. The righteous are alert, perceptive, prudent[121], contemplative, and attentive, with a deep understanding of the consequences of actions. They are filled with wisdom, rationality, determination, virtue, and decisiveness in their proper places.

Therefore, the Quranic discourse is directed to those who possess reason.

Imam 'Alī b. Abī Ṭālib (peace be upon him) said about the traits of the pious: *"Their hallmark is strength in faith,*

---

121. It is for this reason that the terms 'believer' and 'prudent' are often used interchangeably in a number of texts. It is narrated that: "The tongue of the believer is behind their heart." And in some hadiths, it is said: "The tongue of the wise person is behind their heart," because the attributes of the believer and the wise person are identical.

determination with gentleness, belief with certainty, eagerness for knowledge, wisdom with knowledge, moderation in wealth, humility in worship, grace in penury, forbearance in hardship, pursuit of what is lawful, fervour for guidance, and revulsion from desire.

They perform righteous deeds while being cautious, in the evening their concern is gratitude, and in the morning it is remembrance. They spend the night alert and the day joyful—alert to avoid heedlessness and joyful for the grace and mercy they have received. If their soul is burdened with something they dislike, they do not give into its desires. Their eyes find comfort in what does not perish, and their asceticism lies in what is transient. They combine wisdom with knowledge and speech with action.

You will find them hoping for little, slipping rarely, their hearts humble, their souls content, their food simple, their matters easy, their religion safeguarded, their desires dead, their anger restrained. Goodness is expected from them, and their harm is fortuitous. If they are present among the heedless, they are counted among the remembering ones; if they are present among the remembering ones, they are never counted as being from the heedless.

They forgive those who wrong them, give to those who withhold from them, and maintain ties with those who sever relations with them. Obscenity is far-removed from them, their words are gentle, their presence pleasant, and wrongdoing is absent from their deeds. Their goodness is always impending and their evil is always remote. In crises, they remain steadfast, in adversity they are patient, and in ease they are thankful. They do not wrong those they dislike, nor transgress to help those they love. They acknowledge the truth before testimony is given against them, they do not neglect what they are entrusted with, and never forget what they are reminded of. They do not engage in name-calling, nor do they harm their neighbors, nor do they rejoice at others' misfortunes, nor do they engage in misconduct, and they do not stray from the truth.

If they are silent, their silence is not burdensome, and if they laugh, they are not unruly. If wronged, they are patient, Allah Himself avenges them. They castigate themselves into hardship while causing unease to others. They tire themselves for the sake of their Hereafter and give comfort to others by never causing them harm. Their distance from those who avoid them is a sign of their asceticism and purity, while their closeness to those who approach them is marked by kindness and mercy. Their distance is not due to pride or pomposity, and their closeness is not driven by deceit or cunning."[122]

These are the eight principles that represent the foundation of Islamic religious legislation. As for what follows in the legislative texts, they are all applications and details within this broader vision, which may vary based on time, place, and social context. Therefore, one should not elevate the details

---

122. See: *Nahj al-Balāgha*, pg. 305-306.

and applications to the level of fundamental principles of legislation and its general guidance.

Key Matters in Religious Law

Understanding Human Emotions

As for the first topic, human emotions toward various actions and behaviours are not constricted within the scope of noble feelings—which serve as the foundation of legislation—but also include emotions with other origins, some of which may be confused with noble feelings.

Thus, according to the religious perspective that aligns with rational discernment, noble human feelings are susceptible to being mistaken for other types of emotions. This necessitates greater care in identifying the nature of a given emotion and seeking guidance from religion in this matter.

Noble and Habitual Emotions

To clarify: Human emotions are divided into two categories…

The First: Noble emotions represent the innate canon within humans. These emotions serve as the primary source for virtuous and wise legislation. Generally, they are characterised by balance and moderation, ensuring the preservation of public order without leading to negative repercussions.

The Second: Other emotions lean toward excess or deficiency in their contexts. Examples of these include:

1. Feelings of tenderness when they arise from psychological weakness, such as tenderness toward a habitual murderer, or the sentiment of vegetarians toward animals, leading to abstention from eating them.

This category also includes certain maternal tendernesses that manifest in situations requiring firmness, which, if neglected, can significantly harm the child's future. For example, some parents may refuse necessary medical interventions for their children, like amputations of the hand or leg, that are vital to saving the child's life. Similarly, general leniency in enforcing deserved penalties due to misplaced compassion falls into this category. Regarding this, Allah says: {*Do not let compassion for them keep you from carrying out Allah's law, if you truly believe in Allah and the Last Day*}.[123]

Numerous examples illustrate this point, showing that not every feeling of tenderness is virtuous or noble. Instead, some arise from psychological weakness, leading to unfavourable consequences and subsequent harms.

2. Excessive harshness in dealing with minor or slight errors. An example is the undue severity some parents impose

---

123. See: *Sūrat al-Nūr*: 2.

on their children through illegitimate methods, leaving physical and psychological scars.

It is incorrect to view every emotional drive toward preserving a moral value as inherently virtuous. Often, such impulses stem purely from reactive emotions, causing greater harm than the original issue. This is evident in extreme overreactions that exceed the proportionality of their cause from the perspective of divine legislation.

3. Egoism: The egotistic individual perceives and justifies for themselves behaviors and reactions beyond what is permissible. They expect others to bear more responsibilities than they rightfully should, while justifying their own excesses. These emotions are not innate but stem from a desire for superiority and dominance over others, regardless of the means. While the egotistic person may claim such privileges as their right, they view being denied these privileges as an injustice or affront.

4. Desire for equality without acknowledging differences in qualifications: This can manifest in situations such as a lazy student desiring the same grades as a diligent one, accusing the teacher of unfair grading, and feeling wronged or neglected as a result. Similarly, individuals who are at a disadvantage in some capacity—whether due to lack of effort or uncontrollable circumstances such as natural beauty or inherited wealth—may refuse to

accept their situation. This refusal can lead to envy and resentment toward those in better positions, potentially resulting in inappropriate behaviors.

The expectation for equality may also be unfounded. For instance, situations that are misconstrued as favouritism might actually involve differentiated treatment based on distinct needs. An example is a father providing one son with a tool suited to his profession and another son with a different tool appropriate to his work, where the first tool happens to be more expensive. The second son might perceive this as unjust discrimination, even though the difference is tailored to their individual needs rather than inequity.

Similarly, demands for equality between men and women in certain fields overlook the inherent psychological and physical differences between the sexes, which have led to distinct roles and responsibilities being assigned to each.

Ordinary Desires and Noble Feelings

Many ordinary human desires—such as the love of status and wealth—when excessive or overwhelming, may mistakenly be perceived as noble emotions in the process of evaluating them. In other words, a person might erroneously believe that a particular feeling is noble, while in reality, it is a common and insistent urge that demands satisfaction. It appears noble to them, but in essence, it is merely a pressing habitual desire. Modern psychology has clearly observed that human perception is influenced by desires and objectives, a principle that is broadly recognised as self-evident.

It often happens that this false perception obscures reality in the person's conscious mind, and they may become convinced of the validity of their belief. Yet, deep within, they are aware of its inaccuracy. If their innermost self were interrogated, the true nature of the feeling would become apparent.

Even if an individual is unaware of such occurrences within themselves, they can easily recognise this pattern in others. They might observe others clinging to emotions they perceive as noble, which are in fact driven by ordinary desires. This is reflected in the Quranic verse: {*Say [O Prophet], 'shall We inform you of the greatest losers in deeds? * They are those whose effort in the worldly life was misguided, while they assumed they were doing good'*}.[124] Pharaoh's statement about Mūsā also illustrates this phenomenon: {*Let me kill Moses, and let him call upon his Lord, for I fear he may cause you to change your religion, or spread disorder in the land.*}.[125] Furthermore, Pharaoh's words to his people about himself reveal this self-delusion: {*I have told you what I think; I am guiding you to nothing but the right path.*}.[126]

Imām 'Alī (peace be upon him) described the misguided arguments of those who opposed him during the Battle of

---

124. See: *Sūrat al-Kahf*: 103-104.
125. See: *Sūrat Ghāfir*: 26.
126. See: *Sūrat Ghāfir*: 29.

the Camel: *"Every error has its justification, and every defiant person has a pretext."*[127]

Causes of the Second Category of Emotional

The second aforementioned category of emotions—those not genuinely rooted in the human conscience—arise due to several factors, including:

1. Specific psychological traits, such as a psychological weakness that leads to leniency in situations requiring firmness, or an intense disposition that causes excessive severity in situations calling for gentleness.

2. A failure to recognise or fully comprehend the serious consequences of neglecting firmness, or the positive outcomes of gentleness. This results in prioritising immediate and present aspects over future considerations. This notion is reflected in the well-known Arabic adage: "Killing deters killing" a principle confirmed by the Quranic verse: {*And there is for you in legal retribution [saving of] life, O people of understanding*}.[128]

3. The habitual patterns of a person's lifestyle, which make anything deviating from those patterns burdensome.

---

127. See: *Nahj al-Bālagha*, pg. 206.
128. See: *Sūrat al-Baqara*: 179.

For instance, ordinary people often feel uneasy when witnessing a dissection or a surgical operation, as they involve cutting body parts and spilling blood. However, a physician accustomed to seeing and performing such procedures does not share this discomfort. Instead, the physician may feel distress at the thought of leaving the patient untreated, recognising the necessity of surgery to save the patient's life. In this case, the physician's emotion aligns with wisdom, given the clear need for intervention. In contrast, the general public's reaction stems from unfamiliarity and aversion to practices outside the norms they are accustomed to in their daily lives.

Among these examples: Is the aversion many people feel toward slaughtering animals, particularly in our time, where they are accustomed to purchasing pre-slaughtered animals or ready-to-cook meat. However, butchers do not share this sentiment, which aligns with wisdom given the general acceptance of consuming animal meat. Similar examples include the handling of the deceased and engaging in combat with enemies.

Among these examples also: In Western societies, many individuals also show aversion to certain punitive measures, such as the execution of a murderer as retribution for their crime. Although some people are not distressed by such measures—these laws remain in effect in certain states in the U.S.—this aversion may partly stem from their lifestyle, characterised by comfort, luxury, and indulgence, or from a lack of concern for the injustices suffered by others and society due to such crimes. For this reason, such aversion is not typically found among the family members of the victim or those aware of the crime's severe impact on society.

It is noteworthy that some people in Eastern societies imitate such attitudes without possessing the same social or psychological conditions, making their actions seem more like an attempt to blindly mimic.

Among these examples again: Is the absence of human emotions, such as compassion, mercy, and gentleness, in certain individuals. For example, some doctors steal healthy organs from patients, and some warlords disregard the shedding of blood for trivial reasons. This lack of emotion stems from their habitual exposure to cruelty and violence.

4. The failure of individuals to perceive the true abhorrence of certain actions, leading them to regard necessary firmness as excessive or to exaggerate their condemnation of something due to underlying feelings of bias or selfishness...

The first scenario arises when certain immoral acts or widespread vices become normalised within a society. This normalisation could stem from luxury, such as the prevalence of certain ethical violations in modern societies, or from systemic pressures, such as widespread administrative corruption and bribery in some regions due to the absence of effective laws, non-adherence to existing laws, or the difficult living conditions of the people. In such contexts, the inherent abhorrence of these widespread behaviours diminishes in the eyes of individuals within that society, and certain firm measures may be perceived as excessive.

The second scenario is observed in tribal or clan-based societies where some issues are excessively stigmatised, regarded as shameful to the extent that they lead to bloodshed, violations of honour, or the confiscation of property. Such actions might even be based on mere suspicion or assumption. The wrongs committed in response to such stigmatised issues are often far greater in severity than the initial matter that provoked such intense emotions.

5. Exaggeration in reactions is another factor. Extreme emotional responses to certain incidents can lead individuals to deviate from moderation, resulting in either negligence—if the reaction stems from excessive leniency—or extremism—if the reaction is excessively severe.

   This phenomenon occurs within societies as well as among individuals, where a particular incident might provoke a collective reaction characterised by excessive intensity and violence in the opposite direction.

   An example of this: Is the reactions in some Western societies toward Muslims as a result of actions by certain individuals from within the Muslim community that breach human ethical standards and deviate from the bounds of moderation.

The effects of such reactions can linger in the collective memory of a society, persist across subsequent generations, and eventually transform into a cultural norm. This phenomenon might partially explain the negative perception of religion in Western societies, stemming from the hardships they endured during the Middle Ages due to the church's opposition to scientific progress.

6. Imitation: This occurs when certain societies are influenced by others, assuming the latter to be the ideal model, even though the society in question may not have the psychological or social structures to support such a model. An example of this is the influence some individuals in Eastern societies experience from certain phenomena in Western societies, as mentioned previously. Another example is the way successive generations might adopt traditions and norms established by previous generations, even when those norms are based on flawed values.

7. Intellectual Misconceptions: This happens when a person's actions—whether praiseworthy or blameworthy—are attributed to a particular source, but the person receiving the action interprets it through the

lens of a related but separate factor. This can lead to positive or negative emotions toward the action.

An example of this: Is when the negative actions of some individuals who follow a particular religion—stemming from their personal temperaments or erroneous impressions—lead others to develop an aversion to that religion. Similarly, positive behaviours from individuals who adhere to a different religion or philosophical system might attract others to that religion or ideology, even if it lacks a solid intellectual or historical foundation.

Misattributing Nobility to Ordinary Emotions

When examining practical realities, we find that certain intellectual and cultural waves have provided clear examples of attributing noble qualities to certain emotions, even when they are not inherently noble. Some instances include:

1. The Socialist movement that emerged in the previous century and has dominated vast parts of the world for decades, socialism presented itself under inherently human ideals like justice and defending the oppressed. However, in reality, it was a flawed interpretation of human nature, rooted in reactive measures against oppression, feudalism, monopolisation of wealth, and similar issues. Over time, socialism was revealed to be contrary to innate human principles, ultimately leading to its rejection in modern legal and legislative

2. Deviations in marital relationships—which, per human nature, the bodily and psychological structure of relationships is based on the duality of men and women within the framework of family formation. This serves purposes like achieving tranquility, ensuring the preservation of humanity, and safeguarding the next generation. However, in contemporary Western culture, this natural relationship has deviated from its proper course. Pleasure and gratification have been emphasised at the expense of foundational aspects like family formation, role complementarities among its members, and providing a healthy upbringing for future generations. This deviation is often justified through appeals to ostensibly innate values, such as freedom, personal choice and so on.

And what resembles attributing nobility to ordinary emotions is defining noble feelings by part of their supposed scope, due to the dominance of other emotions in the remaining part of it. One example of this can be found in certain aspects of contemporary Western culture, which represent inherent weaknesses according to natural law. For instance, the establishment of human rights within it is based on a social contract, which limits its scope to the boundaries of those countries and does not apply beyond them. As a result, some countries build prisons outside their territories so that they are not subject to their laws, thereby practicing actions that do not align with the natural course of law within those countries.

It has been observed that these countries—which have secured some social rights for their citizens—have, in many cases, acted as colonial powers toward others. They have shown no regard for the lives or resources of these people, and their dealings with others continue to differ sharply from their dealings with their own citizens—in clear violation of the spirit of justice and virtue.

Such a culture and the violations it promotes inevitably lead to collective reactions from the countries or groups affected, resulting in violent movements that see themselves as oppressed and wronged. In such cases, justifying these violations by claiming they do not violate international law is unhelpful. The creators of that law did not act in the interest of the global community as a whole, but rather often considered the political interests of their own countries.

Innate Human Disposition: Simple Yet Complex

It becomes evident from what has been stated that while human nature may seem easy to understand from one perspective, it is, from another perspective, quite elusive. A person may mistakenly believe that certain emotions are innate, and this belief can persist for decades due to the overwhelming waves of emotions generated by clinging to what are thought to be innate values in specific temporal contexts. However, it only becomes clear after applying these emotions in real-life situations that they were not innate after all, revealing their flaws after significant negative consequences.

This highlights the need for human knowledge to be reaffirmed, guided, and assisted, particularly in the realm of legislation, just as is the case in understanding the worldview, as previously discussed.

This leads us to the first topic: Which is the necessity of distinguishing between truly innate principles and other human emotions when sorting through them.

Religious Law and Innate Principles

As for the second topic—concerning the legislative perspective of religion—it is about the extent to which some religious rulings are consistent with the general innate principles.

This is since it may be claimed that some legal rulings contradict the general principles of legislation as referred to earlier, and are in conflict with the defined scope of innate values, and do not belong to the shared space of those principles. Some examples of this include:

Examples of Ambiguous Legislation:

1. Differentiation between males and females in inheritance, or in covering up and *ḥijāb*, and the right to marriage—where a woman's marriage is dependent on the consent of her guardian—and the differentiation between husband and wife in rights and obligations, such as the husband's authority over the household (*qiwāma*), and the permissibility of polygamy. These rulings may be thought to contradict the principle of justice.

2. Certain penal laws concerning crimes, such as the punishment for committing adultery, apostasy, theft, rebellion, and others. These punishments may appear to be harsh and excessive in relation to the offense, and may seem to represent cruelty and severity toward the individual.

   This is in addition to other rulings mentioned in the religious texts or in the legal verdicts (*fatāwa*) of the Muslim jurists...

Clarifying Ambiguous Legislation

To clarify the religious perspective—in general manner—regarding these rulings and the observations about them—without overcomplicating or imposing on the religious texts—it is necessary to mention five points:

1. The necessity of determining the subject of the inquiry in the rulings.

2. The necessity of distinguishing between the level, type, and weight of the ambiguous ruling within the *Sharīʿa*. This requires paying attention to the triad of: Religion, the *Sharīʿa*, and *ijtihādī* jurisprudence.

3. The necessity of observing the general directions and principles in religion that govern the majority of legislative topics.

4. The necessity of caution and avoiding haste in making a definitive claim of the innate judgment being contrary to the presumed legislation, and distinguishing between decisive innate judgements and rational or preliminary preferences.

5. The necessity of verifying the unlikelihood proposed regarding the ambiguous legislations and being mindful of plausible justifications for the ruling, and differentiating between absolute confirmation of a ruling and limited confirmation [of it being in the *Sharīʿa*].

Identifying the Problem in Legislative Matters

As for the First Matter: Its explanation is that not all legislative matters are subject to questioning regarding their conformity with the principles of justice; rather, this is the case for only a portion of them.

To clarify: What is generally questioned among them (i.e. ambiguous legislation) are generally not the fundamental principles or matters of worship, but rather they are some of the branches and applications that may be subject to other *ijtihādī* views, and thus can be correct or erroneous. In this case, the situation does not naturally lead to denying the legitimacy of *Sharīʿa* or undermining confidence in it.

Division of Islamic Legislation

Islamic legislation is divided into principles and objectives, and into branches and applications...

General Principles of Legislation

1. As for the general principles of legislation, they are beyond reproach; because they only aim at seeking the inherent virtues in the manner dictated by their intrinsic value. These principles are not just the foundations of legislation; rather, as previously explained, they form the constitution of *Sharīʿa*, and it is required that legislations pertaining to the branches align with them.[129]

---

129. As has been narrated from Abū ʿAbdillah al-Ṣādiq (peace be upon him), who said: "The Messenger of Allah (peace be upon him and his progeny), said: *'Indeed, for every truth, there is a proof, and upon every correctness, there is light. So,*

It is evident that these principles are matters agreed upon in the divine religions, as evidenced by the verse of Allah: {*He has ordained for you in religion what He enjoined upon Noah, and that which We have revealed to you, and that which We enjoined upon Abraham, Moses, and Jesus: 'Establish the religion and do not divide into factions.' Difficult for the polytheists is that to which you call them*}.[130] This indicates the unity of the laws revealed in the time of Nūḥ and subsequent Prophets.

This includes most of the general prohibitions in their principles, such as the rights of parents, neighbors, kinship, the duty to fulfill oaths and trusts, the obligation to assist the needy, the prohibition of adultery and deviant acts, and the prohibition of harm to others in their lives, bodies, honour, wealth, or reputation—such as mocking, belittling, spying on them, and spreading their secrets—and the prohibition of presenting oneself in a way that causes temptation before others, or exposing oneself to them, and the prohibition of extravagance and waste, and so on.

Division of Religious Branches

2. As for the branches and applications, they are divided into two categories...

---

whatever agrees with the Book of Allah, take it; and whatever contradicts the Book of Allah, leave it.'"See: *al-Kāfī*, Vol. 1, pg. 69.

130. See: *Sūrat al-Shūrā*: 13.

The First Category: Ritual etiquettes, some of which are simple, such as *dhikr* (means of remembrance), supplication, reciting the Holy Book, praise, glorification, seeking forgiveness, whispered prayers with Him (Glorified and Exalted is He), and sharing one's concerns with Him. Some are more complex, consisting of multiple actions, such as prayer, fasting, *Ḥajj*, *'Umra*, visiting mosques, and engaging in *i'tikāf* in them, and the expiations for mistakes and sins.

Distinction of Ritual Etiquette

This section is distinguished from other legislative rulings in the religion by three characteristics that make it of the utmost importance...

The First Characteristic: Ritual etiquette is a manifestation of belief in the great truths affirmed in the religious perspective and the bond between the human being and their Creator, as well as the hereafter. It involves remembering Allah, His attributes, and His greatness, establishing faith in His messages to creation, recalling death and the afterlife, and focusing on the necessity of preparing good deeds for it, drawing from all of these meanings. It has been narrated in a hadith that: *"Prayer is the pillar of religion."*[131]

The Second Characteristic: Ritual etiquette represents the most important and profound human virtues. It is not

---

131. See: *al-Maḥāsin*, Vol. 1, pgs. 44, 286. Also See: *Tahdhīb al-Aḥkām*, Vol. 2, pg. 237.

like other acts of worship, nor is disobedience in it like disobedience in other sins, because in performing it, one submits to Allah, acknowledging His favor and creation, and in disobedience to it, one denies His favor and kindness, as pointed out by religious texts.[132]

---

132. Clarification of this matter: Allah, the Glorified, is the One who bestows upon human beings their existence and every blessing they benefit from, such as the parents, children, spouses, friends, helpers, homes, food, water, trees, animals, the sun, the moon, and more. Thus the relationship of the human being to Allah is comparable to that of a child to their parents or a guest to their host, though with a vast difference. Therefore, we can understand the inappropriate behaviour of a person towards Allah by comparing it to the inappropriate behavior of a child towards their parents. This behaviour may manifest in various ways: At times: It is a matter of disobeying the parents in things they believe are necessary for the child, out of concern for the child's well-being. This is an abhorrent and inappropriate act. At other times: It may involve insulting the parents in a manner that denies the very essence of respect towards them. This could involve the child denying their parents' identity, ascribing falsehoods to them, insulting them with curses, mocking them, or failing to show them basic respect by not greeting them, refusing to visit them, or treating them with contempt in their everyday life. This child would be considered disrespectful to their parents, losing some of the noblest and deepest meanings of humanity, as they deny their origin from which they were born.

In this regard, such degrading behavior cannot be compared to the leniency in obeying other parental commands aimed at the child's welfare, even though it is appropriate to obey them out of their affection for the child. Nor can it be compared to any misdeed towards others, such as committing murder, which is a far more grievous act than the disrespect shown to the parents. The respect that a person owes to their origin, from whom they have received this great blessing, carries the deepest meanings in their soul and demands the utmost care. Denying this respect is an immense injustice. It is easier for a person to remedy this injustice—compared to some of the injustices they may commit towards others, like killing—by asking for forgiveness from the parents and changing their behaviour towards them. In contrast, some major moral wrongs, like killing a respected soul, have no possible means of remedy.

Reflecting on this in the case of a guest and their host: If a person stays as a guest with someone and enjoys their hospitality, benefiting from various blessings and resources over an extended period, it is appropriate to respect the host in a way that reflects the situation. If the guest behaves improperly towards the host, at times this may take the form of failing to accept advice from the host, even if the advice is truly in the best interest of the guest. This is inappropriate, especially if the advice is easy to follow and would actually benefit the guest. At other times, the guest's behavior may involve denying the host's hospitality, as if the provisions and resources provided by the host do not belong to them, or insulting the host, failing to greet them, or treating them disrespectfully. Such actions demonstrate a level of degradation and ugliness that has no parallel in any other behaviour.

This same principle applies to the relationship between Allah, the Exalted, and human beings—with the important distinction that Allah is the Creator of humanity, who has bestowed countless blessings upon them. When a person turns away from submitting to Him, from recognising His

The Third Characteristic: That the acts of worship are the foundation of virtuous and correct behaviour in life, both in the domain of noble values clearly understood by the intellect, such as avoiding harm to others, showing kindness to them, fulfilling promises and trusts, caring for the poor and orphans, maintaining chastity in speech, appearance, and behaviour, and so on... or in the domain where the law has specified the duties.

The reason for this: Is that while the inclination towards virtue is embedded in the human conscience, the belief in Allah (Glorified is He)—as manifested in acts of worship—

---

blessings, and from observing the basic forms of respect towards Him—as if their neglect were an insult—this is a very grievous act.

As the Quran mentions in the wise words of Luqmān: {"*O my son, do not associate anything with Allah. Verily, associating with Allah is a great injustice.*"}See: *Sūrat Luqmān*: 13.
Allah, the Exalted, also says: {*Is the reward for good anything but good?*}See: *Sūrat al-Raḥmān*: 60.
And: {*And should you count the favours of Allah, you could not enumerate them. Indeed, mankind is unjust and ungrateful.*}See: *Sūrat Ibrāhīm*: 34.
Ritual worship are manifestations of etiquette towards Allah, the Exalted. Prayer is a greeting to Him, fasting is an act of discipline in His presence, and the pilgrimage is a visit to His House. How grievous it is for a person to neglect these acts in comparison to their neglect of other commands from Allah, though the latter is also a serious transgression.

and the awareness that He is always with the human being, observing their actions and deeds, and that they will return to their Creator after this life to face the outcome of their actions... This belief stimulates noble motivations and virtue in the human soul and multiplies them many times over.

There is a noteworthy matter regarding these acts of worship...

The Devotional Essence of Worship Across Religions

A. There is, in general, nothing in them that raises questions about their contradiction with natural law, nor is there a place for *ijtihād* that would require changes with time and place, making them part of the mutable aspects of religious law. They are, by their nature, matters that are determined by divine revelation, and the instructions should be followed as they are. It is rare to find anything conflicting with this upon comprehensive reflection.

B. These matters are clearly fixed within this religion without any ambiguity. In fact, in their essence, they belong to the universal divine religion and are common to all religions. Allah says: {*And We inspired to them the doing of good deeds and the establishment of prayer*}.[133] And He said: {*and He enjoined upon me the prayer and the alms so long*

---

133. See: *Sūrat al-Anbiyā'*: 73.

as I am alive].[134] He also said: {*Fasting has been decreed upon you as it was decreed upon those before you*}.[135]

Yes, there are detailed matters of *ijtihād* that may be subject to flexibility when no definitive evidence is available, or in cases where one follows any clear juristic opinion.

Matters Unrelated to Worship

The Second Category: Matters unrelated to worship, such as rulings on foods, including what is prohibited and restricted; financial obligations like the *zakāt* (alms) and *khums*; rulings on financial transactions among people, including trade and leasing; personal status laws concerning marriage, divorce, waiting periods, inheritance, and wills; judicial laws and testimonies; rulings on blood money; and penal laws, including *qiṣāṣ* (retribution), prescribed punishments, and discretionary penalties.

As for these rulings:

Some of them: Are matters that do not inherently raise questions about their alignment with wisdom or innate human disposition—whether in themselves or specifically in this era. This category constitutes the majority of such rulings.

---

134. See: *Sūrat Maryam*: 31.
135. See: *Sūrat al-Baqara*: 183.

the second reason is that we are not talking to a person who does not believe in GOD A here. A person who believes in God

And some of them: Are matters that have raised questions about their compatibility with clear principles of one's innate disposition and human conscience.

This category includes rulings that are subject to *ijtihād* and others that are definitive (*qaṭʿī*). However, in most cases, these rulings allow for differing perspectives within scholarship[136]—

---

136. This is for one of the following reasons:
    A. Some of these rulings may have evidence and indicators that usually lead to certainty or reassurance, but they do not lead to that when it is proven that they contradict the innate human disposition. This is because the evidence, which would usually lead to certainty, may not lead to actual certainty due to its opposition by stronger evidence that leaves no room for doubt.
    B. Some of these rulings are nothing more than *ijtihādī* evidence, and it is not correct to act upon *ijtihādī* evidence when its content is proven to be incorrect due to its contradiction with a decisive proof—whether from reason or clear textual evidence that leaves no room for doubt.
    C. Some of these rulings, although they are a fixed part of the law in principle due to clear and obvious evidence, their continuation depends on *ijtihād*. This is because their continuation relies on either temporal absoluteness and the presumption of no abrogation, or on the ruling being an initial one, not one of authority, depending on the type of evidence that supports this. Alternatively, it may rely on the general nature of the ruling and its lack of restriction in a way that would cause it to differ depending on circumstances and conditions.

particularly within certain expansive methodologies—such as the *maqāṣid*-oriented approach to jurisprudence, as will be explained later.

Definitive and Ambiguous Rulings

The Second Matter: One important consideration that is incumbent for a person to note regarding ambiguous religious rulings that have been questioned for their compatibility with innate human disposition, is the need to distinguish between the level of certainty of the ruling, its type, and its weight within the framework of *Sharīʿa*.

Distinguishing Religion, Sharīʿa, and Jurisprudence

This requires distinguishing between three key concepts: Religion, *Sharīʿa*, and Interpretive Jurisprudence (*fiqh ijtihādī*). This tripartite classification, along with its specific features, is one of the most critical aspects of understanding the outline of the religion.

1. As explained earlier, the essence of religion, represents a worldview grounded in the triad of: The Creator, His message to humanity, and the human's existence after death. These are the unchanging tenets of religion that, from a religious perspective, have existed since the creation of humanity. Clear and definitive evidence and arguments support them, leaving no room for renewal, change, or differing interpretations. As Allah states: {*He*

has ordained for you in religion what He enjoined upon Noah, and that which We have revealed to you, and that which We enjoined upon Abraham, Moses, and Jesus: 'Establish the religion and do not divide into factions.' Difficult for the polytheists is that to which you call them}.¹³⁷

2. As for the *Sharīʿa*, this refers to the legislative teachings that are genuinely issued by the Islamic Lawgiver, regardless of whether they have been fully conveyed to people or not.

These teachings are established for us in what is conveyed clearly and unequivocally, without requiring specialised effort (*ijtihād*) that could involve error or correctness. Examples include the explicit legislative commands found in the Quran and reliably transmitted Sunna, such as the fundamental obligations of prayer, pilgrimage (*Ḥajj*), and the alms (*Zakāt*).

This category of teachings, established with certainty and which is free of doubt, can be termed "legislative truths" because of their definitive nature.

3. As for Interpretive jurisprudence (*fiqh ijtihādī*), then this consists of rulings derived by jurists using the available interpretive tools, which do not establish rulings with definitive certainty. Instead, alternative theories with

---

137. See: *Sūrat al-Shūrā*: 13.

their own evidentiary support exist, as is common in matters of scholarly disagreement. There may also be hypotheses that cannot be categorically negated.

This category can be referred to as "legislative theories" because, while they are substantiated by valid argumentation and thus mandate adherence, they do not attain the level of definitive religious truths.

This category—which is susceptible to correctness and error—should not be attributed to *Sharīʿa* with absolute certainty, nor should the religion and *Sharīʿa* be fully defined by its conclusions. Instead, it reflects the conclusions reached through the interpretive tools available to jurists. Some jurists may possess a deeper understanding of *Sharīʿa*, its objectives, and its rulings than others. Additionally, certain juristic arguments may not always provide definitive proof but instead offer strong indications, which necessitate adherence unless clear evidence of their error emerges. Some legal tools function as procedural guidelines to clarify practical obligations rather than establishing definitive rulings of the *Sharīʿa*.[138]

---

138. To clarify this: *Ijtihādī* jurisprudence is of several types:
 The First: What some jurists or a group of them or many of them are certain about, but this does not make it certain at the level of knowledge. Rather, it has indicators upon which a jurist may be certain, while another jurist may act upon it as evidence, allowing for other possible hypotheses.
 The Second: What is supported by signs and evidence that lead to reassurance, without definitively ruling out the

Therefore, if an aspect of this category definitively and conclusively contradicts principles of justice, this contradiction itself serves as evidence that the interpretive argument supporting it is flawed and that an alternative interpretive approach must be pursued.

Considering Religious Values in Judgment

The Third Matter: Every legislative system is naturally comprised of principles and general directions where when applied result in detailed rulings. Consequently, rulings in specific cases generally represent the application of these overarching principles and directions. Thus, when analysing a specific position, it is crucial for researchers to begin with

---

possibility of error.

The Third: What is supported by probable evidence that is accepted, such as the apparent meaning of speech, which is a binding legal evidence in all positive laws, even though it is open to disagreement. Such evidence usually leads to probability, although it may not necessarily result in probability in every instance, even though it is considered evidence in cases where there is no probability perceived by the one reviewing it.

The Fourth: What determines the legal stance as a practical function in cases of doubt, such as not acting on an obligation based merely on a possibility, and maintaining the previous ruling until evidence contrary to it is established. This is referred to in contemporary legal theory as "practical functions (*al-waẓā'if al-'amaliyya*)."

explicit general principles and established rules, progressing systematically to the particular matter under consideration.

This method ensures clarity on whether the supposed position represents a foundational principle or a general direction, or whether it is an isolated or exceptional case necessitated by specific factors. Researchers must also ascertain the expected framework for addressing it legislatively, as well as the level of certainty regarding the position when it appears inconsistent with established, definitive principles and general certainties.

Ambiguous Cases and Their Limits in Defining Religion

When observing the legislative examples that might be claimed to conflict with the general innate principles, it becomes evident that these instances cannot define the overarching character and general orientation of religion and religious legislation. Instead, they must be understood within the context of the specific circumstances or facts that are fixed and or subject to change that the religious legislation considers, as will be further elaborated.

The foundation of religious legislation, as outlined in its texts, lies in the observance of established human values, referred to in the language of the evidence as *"ma'rūf"* (what is known as good) and *"munkar"* (what is recognised as bad). This principle was not merely a slogan employed by religion to attract followers; rather, it is, from its perspective, a fundamental condition for the authenticity of its message. The mark of the Prophet of Islam's truthfulness was his enjoining of good and forbidding of evil, and religion views legislative justice as an essential, immutable attribute of Allah, akin to His justice in reward and retribution.

This is further clarified by the numerous emphases on noble moral values in the Quranic texts across various contexts, such as:

1. Allah being described as affectionate to people, compassionate, merciful, forgiving, forbearing, grateful, kind, ever-relenting, fulfilling promises, and not breaking them. He is not unjust to His servants.

2. In describing His Messengers, He said about His Prophet, Muḥammad (peace be upon him and his progeny): {*Indeed, you are of great moral character*}[139] and {*There has certainly come to you a Messenger from among yourselves. Your suffering distresses him: he is deeply concerned for you and full of kindness and mercy towards the believers.*}[140] He also says: {*So by mercy from Allah, [O Muhammad], you were lenient with them. And if you had been rude [in speech] and harsh in heart, they would have disbanded from you*}[141] Furthermore, He states:

---

139. See: *Sūrat al-Qalam*: 4.
140. See: *Sūrat al-Tawba*: 128.
141. See: *Sūrat Āl ʿImrān*: 159.

{*Do not let yourself perish over them in regrets*}¹⁴² and: {*Perhaps you would kill yourself with grief that they will not be believers*}.¹⁴³ Similarly, other Prophets are described with noble attributes such as righteousness, truthfulness, patience, wisdom, and kindness to their parents.

3. Allah loving the beneficent, the patient, the just, the repentant, and the pious. He does not love the transgressors, the unjust, the treacherous, the arrogant, or those who are boastful or sinful.

4. In the context of articulating the general legislative principles, Allah states: {*Indeed, Allah commands justice, good conduct, and giving to relatives and forbids obscenity, bad conduct, and oppression*}.¹⁴⁴ And also: {*Indeed, Allah does not command obscenity*}.¹⁴⁵

It should be noted that these legislative principles, from the religious perspective, are not merely theoretical foundations without practical applications. Rather, they are:

Firstly: Independent legislative provisions in and of themselves at a general level. The obligation of justice, the virtue of benevolence, and similar principles are general legislative rulings. Moreover, Islam in numerous specific

---

142. See: *Sūrat Fāṭir*: 8.
143. See: *Sūrat al-Shuʿarāʾ*: 3.
144. See: *Sūrat al-Naḥl*: 90.
145. See: *Sūrat al-Aʿrāf*: 28.

rulings has relied on a general innate principle, such as the command for husbands to treat their wives with kindness.

Secondly: They represent legislative objectives, serving as indicators of the boundaries of other legislations on one hand, and as the general framework for what should guide the governance of rulers, governors, and jurists in areas where they are authorised to judge and exert discretion on the other. Thus, these principles possess an inexhaustible legislative content.

5. Furthermore, Islam has taken a clear direction in its specific legislations aimed at eliminating injustice and oppression and establishing justice, especially concerning vulnerable groups such as women, slaves, and orphans. It has also focused on regulating groups prone to arbitrariness or injustice, such as tribal leaders driven by prejudice, impassioned fighters, and wronged individuals who might lean towards excessive retaliation.

6. Regarding the legislation and propagation of the message, it is evident that Islam approached people with kindness and consideration. A study of the history of Islamic legislation reveals the extent of gradualism and accommodation in conveying the religion and expanding its rulings. This gradual approach was among the reasons why the Messengers were chosen from those distinguished by patience, forbearance, humility, and care for people.

7. On dealing with adversaries, the religion demonstrates adherence to principles of justice—particularly maintaining trust and honouring agreements—even with enemies, except in cases requiring firmness. Notable examples include obliging Muslims to honour their treaties with polytheists and prohibiting aggression against them, as well as forbidding the breach of covenants unless there is clear evidence of their deceit against Muslims. Even then, the annulment of treaties must be declared openly, ensuring that adversaries are not caught off guard by sudden attacks. Allah says: {*Fight in the way of Allah those who fight you, but do not transgress. Indeed, Allah does not like transgressors*}.[146]

8. On the practical level, there is no doubt that when Islam is implemented by the Imams of the religion, it ensures a significant qualitative shift toward social justice, as becomes evident through close examination of the life of the Prophet (peace be upon him and his progeny) and his Ahl al-Bayt (peace be upon them).

9. On nurturing the Muslim individual, Islamic pedagogy for shaping the Muslim character is rooted in fostering wisdom and virtue. This is evident in the sermons of Imam ʿAlī (peace be upon him) delivered from the pulpit of Kūfa directed at the general populace, his letters to Mālik al-Ashtar and Muḥammad b. Abī Bakr,

---

146. See: *Sūrat al-Baqara*: 190.

his directives to his son al-Ḥasan (peace be upon him), as well as his maxims, exhortations, and admonitions. Remarkably, this was achieved in an era that was far from tranquil or stable, instead it was rife with turmoil, strife, wars, and the well-known and diverse forms of conflict.

From what has been mentioned: It becomes clear that religion generally starts from general and wise principles, and from this, two matters follow:

The First: When it is established that there is a clear contradiction between a well-known ruling and instinct or wisdom, this in itself becomes a proof against that ruling, necessitating the direction towards the opposite ruling. In this case, it is not correct to insist that religion and the law are bound to this ruling, because the religious texts themselves base the religious law on consideration of wisdom and virtue, a principle agreed upon by the jurists. If reason concludes that a certain ruling contradicts its definitive principles, this in itself negates the possibility that this ruling is part of the divine law, as the divine ruling cannot contradict rational judgment. Therefore, another legislative direction must be followed in dealing with the matter.

Even if this legislative direction is excluded from a jurisprudential perspective, the comparison between its exclusion and the weight of religion and the repeated proofs of its teachings is inappropriate. It is not logical to disregard this truth—proven by its repeated evidence—unless the possibility of another valid approach arises, even if it is not immediately obvious. This is what is referred to as a "potential unknown," which will be further clarified in the discussion of Innate Principles for Verification, God-Willing.

The Second: It is not correct to consider the aforementioned resources—in cases where they have been definitively proven—as indicative of a characteristic of discrimination or harshness in the religion. This is similar to a situation where one observes good behaviour, kindness, and ethics in a person but sometimes sees actions that seem to contradict that. It is not the case that these negative actions should be seen as the general behaviour of the individual.

Limits of Human Reason in Understanding Divine Law

There is no doubt that religion takes into account reason and is based on rational constants, but this does not mean that reason can fully grasp everything that religion teaches. There may be areas where reason either halts or has doubts about the logic of certain matters.

This is true of all laws that aim to follow natural wisdom and principles. Not everyone is able to understand the reasoning and wisdom behind all rulings. A sound natural logic dictates that a person, when confident about something, should rely on what they know to be true, rather than letting doubts or speculations cloud their judgment in uncertain areas. This is well-known and has been practiced by rational individuals in all areas of life.

For example, if a person trusts a certain doctor's skill and competence, reason dictates that they should follow the doctor's advice and not give weight to doubts or second-guess the doctor's expertise in areas where they feel unsure. Similarly, if a son learns wisdom through experience with his father, the natural thing is to trust his father's opinion when there is a seeming contradiction, because the father's experience holds more weight.

Thus, it can be said that religion—according to its view—is committed to justice and is not opposed to instinct in all the previous cases, but it offers a particular perspective in its legislative view, according to the religious legislation it carries.

Caution in Opposing Assumed Legislation

The Fourth Matter: It is important, in the context of ambiguous legislation, not to hastily claim a definitive natural judgment that contradicts the presumed legislation. Adequate verification is necessary, as we often observe that a person may initially judge a situation as naturally reprehensible to act against but later retracts this view after encountering subsequent complications or new insights, as we have previously noted in some examples.

Here, we suffice with mentioning two critical points related to this matter:

Definitive Judgments and Reasonable Estimations

The First Point: It is crucial to differentiate between definitive natural judgments and other rational estimations that do not reach the level of definitive certainty.

When a person reflects on the decisions they make with the intention of achieving noble objectives such as justice, fairness, truthfulness, chastity, or other requisites for individual and social well-being, these decisions can be classified into two types:

The First Type: Those characterised by definitive certainty. In such cases, the individual perceives the situation with clarity and understands all elements that could influence and affect the decision. Here, there is no possibility of any repercussions, outcomes, or new information that could shift the well-formed intellect from its proposed decision.

The scholars of Legal Theory (*al-Uṣūliyyūn*) refer to this type of stance as "rational judgments (*al-aḥkām al-'aqliyya*)".

The Second Type: Those that are not characterised by definitive certainty but rather represent reasonable approaches based on available and accessible information. These decisions cannot guarantee permanence, as they are subject to change upon further understanding of the consequences of what currently seems to be a correct decision.

Such situations, which may initially appear correct to a person, are valid to act upon given the individual's current level of knowledge, provided no evidence contradicts them. However, it is incorrect to label these judgments as definitive, certain, fixed, or unchanging. Describing them in such terms would constitute exaggeration, overconfidence, and ignorance.

The scholars of Legal Theory refer to this type of judgment and assessment as "rational estimations" (*al-aḥkām al-ʿaqliyya*) or "rational fixations" (*al-murtakazāt al-ʿaqliyya*) and regard them as the foundation of human behavior in the absence of an authoritative religious text. Their validity is contingent upon the absence of definitive evidence opposing them, as they inherently lack absolute certainty and are therefore susceptible to error.

It appears that the majority of human decisions fall into this category, as can be observed by examining the decisions individuals make, whether these are societal decisions stemming from political or social positions, such as those made by heads of state, or personal decisions concerning one's own affairs, family, and children, or judgments about matters involving others.

This becomes even clearer when decisions are reviewed after some time, once their effects and consequences have unfolded, and all aspects of the matter have been fully revealed. At that point, alternative options often become apparent, options that might have been closer to justice, wisdom, and prudence. Consequently, a person may reflect on such situations and say: {*If I had knowledge of the unseen, I would have reaped much good*}[147] or: "If I were to go back to the beginning of this matter with the knowledge I have now, I would have handled it differently."

For this reason, people are advised to consider the opinions and experiences of others, exercise caution in matters, and avoid hastiness in judgment. This advice, often directed toward young people, is particularly relevant even when a young person is motivated by noble sentiments and worthy goals such as justice, fairness, righteousness, support for truth, alleviation of harm, and kindness to others. Even so, those who have gained life experience often see that such youthful approaches are flawed and may lead to regret in the future.

When examining the perspective of scholars and experts, it becomes clear that they anticipate and consider possibilities that the general public—even specialists—might overlook or dismiss. This is because they analyse matters from a higher vantage point, observing historical events both ancient and modern, considering the psychological and social

---

147. See: *Sūrat al-A'rāf*: 188.

dimensions of various choices, and comparing cases and their parallels across different circumstances. They scrutinise the implications and outcomes of unusual and rare events, delve into past and present intellectual and cultural trends and their potential future implications, and give thought to unrealised possibilities just as much as they do to those that have already occurred. Numerous modern psychological studies have touched on aspects of these concepts, though the topic itself remains vast and profound.

Scholars often employ hypothetical scenarios to challenge entrenched patterns of human thought and to dismantle many fixed ideas and impressions that people hold as certainties. For example, one might consider the hypothetical return of 'Isā b. Maryam (peace be upon him), as awaited by Christians, performing miracles that defy the natural order and shake human understanding—just as he did during his first mission. Would the majority of people not then submit to his message and to the values and laws he establishes from Allah, even if they conflict with prevailing cultural norms?

Similarly, if the Mahdī awaited by Muslims were to appear—a devout servant of Allah, guided by Him, restoring the principles of religion that have been distorted or obscured—accompanied by extraordinary signs that compel universal acknowledgment, would the widespread impressions and deeply held views not be dismantled if he refuted them?

Among the reminders of this is the observable divergence among those described as rational and inclined to pursue wisdom when assessing what constitutes justice, integrity, chastity, and other virtues. This divergence becomes apparent to researchers who examine differences in civil laws across various countries regarding numerous detailed issues with complex dimensions, such as capital punishment, investigative methods with criminals and suspects, and educational or social approaches. What one group may describe as unjust might be considered by others to align with justice and public welfare. If one were to compile and analyse the disparities in laws and the perspectives of rational individuals on legislative topics and their associated issues, this discrepancy would become abundantly clear.

The point here is not to create an atmosphere of doubt that leads to a lack of trust in the human perspective altogether—such an approach would be an unreasonable extreme. Rather, the aim is to cultivate mature insights and retain a proper sense of proportion and context. Personal reflections or cultural waves should not be elevated to the level of immutable certainties that represent absolute truth, unaffected by any new information, consequences, or alternative thought processes.

Accordingly, researchers must acknowledge that many judgements they perceive as definitive rational conclusions, immune to debate or alteration, may not actually hold such an unassailable position in reality. At best, these are reasoned perspectives that may be accurate or flawed.

Thus, it is inappropriate to treat such views as challenges to the definitive, established principles of religion and the *Sharī'a*. Even more so, they should not be used to cast doubt on the intellectual framework of religion, with its substantial weight, evidential basis, and foundational principles.

Differentiating Similar Concepts

(The Second Point): This emphasises the need to differentiate between similar and closely related concepts, avoiding conflating them, as often happens with initial impressions of a topic. Two examples illustrate this:

Distinguishing Justice from Equality

The First Example: Is the differentiation between justice and equality. Equality demands uniformity in the outcome of rulings, regardless of the differences between those judged. For instance, equality between two workers in wages would entail giving both the same salary, regardless of differences in their contributions.

Justice, however, does not necessarily require equality. Instead, it involves assessing each matter according to its true value. For example, if one worker performs a task of greater value than the other—such as a doctor's hour of work compared to a labourer's hour spent carrying heavy objects—

then evaluating each according to their contributions, even if it leads to disparity, is in fact itself justice.

Considering justice as identical to equality is a common misconception among people.

This distinction also applies to the differing rulings for men and women. In the religious perspective, men and women are not entirely equal or identical in their creation. Each fulfills a distinct and complementary role. Consequently, this natural differentiation leads to varying duties and responsibilities, reflected in religious rulings. The issue becomes problematic and stirs emotions when men misuse their rights oppressively, or when women seek to emulate men in their characteristics without acknowledging that this differentiation stems from natural differences between the genders.

Due to their delicate constitution and deep emotions, women are more vulnerable to the consequences of appearing in alluring ways before men, as is evident from social realities. This consideration appears to underpin the requirement of *ḥijāb* for women.[148]

---

148. As stated in the verse of *Ḥijāb*: {*O Prophet, tell your wives and your daughters and the women of the believers to bring down over themselves part of their outer garments. That is more suitable that they will be known and not be abused. And ever is Allah Forgiving and Merciful.*}See: *Sūrat al-Aḥzāb*: 59.

In general, this differentiation is clear and natural. Many parents in Western countries feel significant discomfort with the behaviours of their daughters compared to their sons, even though their culture does not support addressing such concerns.[149]

Distinction Between Firmness and Severity

The Second Example: Is the distinction between firmness and deterrence on the one hand, and severity on the other, when reflecting on the foundations of the penal rulings. Every legislation is based on two pillars: Adopting leniency and its requisites of compassion, mercy, and mitigation, and adopting firmness and its requisites of insistence, steadfastness, and resolve.

Each of these pillars has its appropriate place according to the measure of wisdom. When taken beyond its proper bounds, the result is counterproductive. Just as leniency in its place can have profound positive effects, firmness in its rightful position can yield similar, if not greater, benefits. It can

---

149. Nevertheless, it cannot be denied that women may face injustice under the pretext of tribal customs or personal motives of certain men, though the inverse may also occur. However, the religious perspective does not stem from belittlement or domination, rather, from the recognition of differences in physical and psychological constitution, which result in differing familial and societal roles assigned to each party.

correct a person's life path and prevent crimes in hundreds or thousands of instances where they might otherwise occur.

The justification for penal rulings in the religious perspective—affirming the rational and innate perspective—is not merely retaliation for violating a commandment or satisfying the spirit of vengeance in the aggrieved.[150] Rather, the justification lies in the prescribed punishment serving as a societal deterrent against crime, provided it does not exceed the bounds of proportional justice with the offense, considering its degree of immorality according to innate standards. For example, retribution (*qiṣāṣ*) against a murderer is a just punishment for the crime of killing, as highlighted in the Quran: {*And there is for you in legal retribution [saving of] life, O people of understanding*}.[151] It serves as a deterrent against killing and is proportional to the crime because it is a punishment in kind. Allah states: {*And We ordained for them in it [the Torah]: a life for a life, an eye for an eye, a nose for a nose, an ear for an ear, a tooth for a tooth, and for wounds [a proportionate] retaliation*}.[152] This indicates that

---

150. In reality, the basic drive for vengeance—generally speaking—can be considered one of the innate emotions that fulfills the interest of social deterrence at a collective level. If humans were entirely devoid of this spirit and naturally inclined toward forgiveness and pardon in all circumstances, criminals would feel secure from punishment, and crime would multiply.
151. See: *Sūrat al-Baqara*: 179.
152. See: *Sūrat al-Mā'ida*: 45.

the ruling of equal retribution aligns with what innate human nature dictates within its clear boundaries. Therefore, it is a ruling shared by all divine laws, not a specific act of devotion exclusive to Islamic law.

The religious texts emphasise the principle of proportionality between the crime and the punishment in cases where individuals transgress against one another, as illustrated in the verse: {*So whoever transgresses against you, transgress against them in a similar manner to what they transgressed against you*}.[153] For this reason, religion does not permit the aggrieved party to exceed the level of retribution by even the slightest measure, even though human nature tends toward intensifying the punishment for the crime—because, as the saying goes: "The initiator [of injustice] is the greater wrongdoer."

This highlights that in the religious perspective, the rationale behind the prescribed punishments for certain crimes is that they represent a form of proportional firmness, which is more favourable in its consequences than leniency, for several reasons:

1. Its significant impact in deterring individuals from committing such crimes and elevating them above these actions, while leniency and laxity lead to substantial

---

153. See: *Sūrat al-Baqara*: 194.

moral, ethical, and cognitive breakdowns within society, accompanied by vile and base behaviors.

2. The potential for leniency to provoke extreme reactions within the social environment, which may exceed the severity of the punishment imposed by the religious law, particularly when those transgressions contradict the fundamental values and virtuous principles respected by the community.

3. The necessity of leniency would require punishing hundreds of individuals with lighter penalties instead of punishing a single individual with a firm and proportionate punishment for the crime committed. This is because reducing the deterrent effect increases the likelihood of crime occurring, leading to frequent application of lenient punishments, whereas strong deterrence reduces the occurrence of crimes and, consequently, the need to apply severe punishments.

Some people may perceive certain punishments as harsh for several reasons.

Among them: Is the lack of proper understanding of the severity and gravity of certain crimes.

And Among them: Is their innate sense of tenderness towards practices that may seem harsh, even if necessitated by wisdom and foresight.

And Among them: Is focusing solely on the punishment itself while disregarding its broader societal benefits, such as preserving people's lives, honour, and property, as well as maintaining public order.

And Among them: Is the ignorance of many people regarding the severe harm and large-scale corruption caused by violations and transgressions, which often lead to infringements on essential rights such as life, honour, and property. They may also fail to recognise the role firm punishments play in preventing these harms. For instance, drivers who frequently violate traffic laws may view strict traffic regulations and associated fines as unnecessary restrictions, not realising the significant number of injuries and fatalities resulting from such violations.

Thus, it is unwise to hastily judge any punishment as inconsistent with the principles of justice when it comes to penal rulings.

Moreover, a closer examination of punishments prescribed in divine law for prohibitions categorised as violations of Allah's rights reveals an approach that emphasises deterrence. Severe punishments are outlined but are paired with stringent conditions for establishing guilt and proving the crime. This often leads to these punishments being rarely enforced, creating a strong deterrent effect without widespread application, thereby discouraging open criminal behavior while limiting the need for frequent implementation.[154]

---

154. For instance, consider the punishment of flogging for fornication (*fāḥisha*). The eligibility for this punishment is not based on the mere establishment of the act through indicators or evidence that might lead to certainty, such as frequenting a woman who is not related to the man or engaging in suspicious behavior. It is not even sufficient if they are seen together in an inappropriate situation. Instead, the punishment requires the testimony of four witnesses who explicitly attest to having seen the physical act clearly. This means, in practical terms, that the punishment is effectively imposed only when the act reaches the level of public exposure, to the extent that it becomes evident to four upright (*'ādil*) individuals without any attempt by the perpetrators to conceal it.

Had the punishment been predicated solely on the act of fornication itself, it would suffice for the judge to rely on indicators that establish certainty—just as is the practice in modern legal systems concerning what they classify as prohibited criminal acts.

It is apparent that this condition in Islamic law imposes an extremely stringent requirement for proving fornication, especially when considering that this ruling was revealed in an Arab society characterised by a strong sense of protective jealousy (*ghīra*), where accusations of such acts were made based on the slightest suspicion or doubt. In such a society, reactions to perceived impropriety—such as seeing a man leave a woman's house—were often immediate and violent, such as through acts of murder.

Moreover, Islam did not limit itself to requiring a rare level of proof for establishing guilt; it also prescribed a punishment of flogging for anyone who accuses another of fornication without producing four witnesses who meet the aforementioned conditions. This measure creates a deterrent effect, discouraging people from making such

Absolute and Limited Establishment of Rulings

The Fifth Matter: When reflecting on seemingly ambiguous legislative examples, it is necessary to distinguish between the absolute establishment of a ruling and its limited establishment. This distinction encompasses three scenarios...

Comprehensive and Restricted Legislation

The First Scenario: Is the necessity of differentiating between comprehensive legislation and restricted legislation. Comprehensive legislation might provoke questions and doubts that restricted legislation does not, particularly when considering its limitations, which can clarify the reasonable considerations underlying the proposed legislation.

---

accusations for fear that some witnesses might retract their statements or testify only to proximity or contact rather than the explicit physical act, which is often difficult to observe.

Thus, the requirement stipulated in Islam for proving fornication practically prevents its establishment except in rare instances. According to these stringent conditions, fornication is unlikely to be proven in more than a single case among a large number of occurrences.

This clearly indicates that Islam's policy on fornication focuses on instilling fear of committing the act by emphasising the public and explicit nature of its proof. This approach seeks to prevent fornication from becoming a publicly acknowledged phenomenon that could corrupt the social atmosphere. To achieve this, Islam restricts the avenues for proving the act and imposes severe penalties for publicly accusing others of it.

For instance, consider the differentiation in inheritance between males and females who share the same type of kinship, such as children or siblings. This differentiation is not universal; rather, it applies specifically to the paternal relatives of the deceased, such as their male and female children or their paternal brothers and uncles. In contrast, maternal relatives, like maternal siblings, inherit equally, as explicitly stated in the verse on maternal kinship (*kalālat al-umm*): {*And if a man or woman dies leaving neither ascendants nor descendants but has a brother or a sister, then for each of them is one-sixth. But if they are more than two, they share equally in a third*}.[155] This is undisputed amongst the jurists of the Muslims.

It seems that the reason for favouring males among paternal relatives lies in their traditional role as the deceased's clan. They were expected to protect the deceased's children and assume responsibility for blood money (*diyya*) if required. This arrangement aligns with a system of reciprocal rights and obligations among paternal relatives, akin to a form of mutual insurance within the paternal kinship network.

Variable and Fixed Rulings in Islamic Law

The Second Scenario: It is essential to differentiate between the variable and fixed rulings in Islamic law. A ruling may represent a reasonable measure of justice in a specific

---

155. See: *Sūrat al-Nisā'*: 12.

historical context but may no longer hold the same adequacy in a different era.

This concept is, broadly speaking, clear and self-evident. It would not be reasonable for one to label previous generations as entirely unjust for engaging in practices now considered objectionable. Those generations adhered to natural principles (*fiṭra*) within the limits of human understanding and awareness at the time. For instance, one cannot accuse our forefathers of being oppressive in their methods of disciplining children; their actions were not driven by mere impulsiveness. Rather, their disciplinary measures were reasonable within the constraints of their culture—provided they did not violate innate principles—and were informed by their perception of wisdom at the time, including their consideration of the consequences of lesser forms of punishment. However, such practices may not align with contemporary standards.

Therefore, believing that certain actions or practices have always constituted oppression from the dawn of humanity until the present—without regard for cultural contexts, environments, circumstances, norms, traditions, and available alternatives—is to be regarded as naïve and immature thinking.

The scientific and technical reasoning behind this differentiation lies in the recognition that innate principles, while constant in their general foundations within the human conscience, may vary in their applications, tools of implementation, and supportive customs depending on time and circumstances. This understanding is well-established among scholars of sociology and law.

Thus, it becomes clear that a ruling that aligns with natural principles in one society or era may not hold the same alignment in another. If a ruling in the *sharī'a* is determined to be among the variable aspects, there is no issue or contradiction in this realisation.[156]

---

156. Two important clarifications regarding the origins of changes in rulings and distinguishing between the fixed and variable:
The First Clarification: Regarding the origins of changes in rulings, there are three primary causes for changes in Islamic jurisprudence and law:
The First: Abrogation of the ruling by the legislator: This entails a direct replacement or modification of a ruling through divine revelation.
The Second: Governance-based rulings (*wilā'ī rulings*): These are rulings issued by the ruler or governing authority based on changing interests across different times and places. Every legal system includes fixed elements while also allowing for discretionary legislation by the state in response to dynamic interests, provided these adhere to overarching principles of legislation. Thus, if a ruling is determined to have been issued by the authority based on legal jurisdiction, it can later be amended by the same authority without being classified as abrogation in the technical sense. For example, a ruler determining an appropriate discretionary punishment (*ta'zīr*) for certain offenses.
Jurists may differ regarding whether certain rulings fall

under primary (i.e. fixed) legislation or governance-based (*wilā'ī*) rulings subject to change.

The Third: Contextually rooted limitations of the initial ruling: The primary ruling might be inherently restricted by contextual factors recognised by legal scholars familiar with the general principles of the legislative system and the specific aspects considered in that legislation. This limitation might result in the ruling not applying when circumstances and context shift.

For example, the principle that combatants are entitled to personal spoils from the battlefield was based on the historical nature of warfare, where fighters individually prepared and equipped themselves. This principle would not logically extend to modern warfare contexts where the state provides all preparation and equipment. Thus, it would be unreasonable to extend this ruling to situations involving the seizure of modern assets like tanks, aircraft, or artillery.

The Second Clarification: Concerning the means of determining between whether a ruling is fixed or variable in the *Sharī'a*, there are two primary methodologies:

1. Text-Based Approach: This method strictly adheres to the explicit textual sources, treating all mentioned rulings as inherently fixed legislative commands.
2. Purpose-Based Approach (*Maqāṣid al-Fiqh*): This method interprets the intent and objectives underlying legislative texts within the framework of general principles of Islamic law. Based on this interpretation, it delineates boundaries for textual rulings, allowing for adjustments to rulings in response to temporal and spatial changes.

Within this purpose-based approach, there are several perspectives, some of which greatly expand the scope of legislative purposes and consider many traditionally fixed rulings to be variable.

These methodologies agree on three foundational rules for deriving rulings...

The First Rule: Not all rulings are universally applicable across all times. This is not due to any authority to abrogate the rulings, but because some were fundamentally governance-based or contextually limited. An example is the aforementioned ruling on spoils of war.

Therefore, anyone deriving legislative positions must take this reality into account.

The Second Rule: The default assumption is the stability of rulings. Any claim of change must be substantiated with clear evidence. It is insufficient to base such claims on mere personal inclinations or speculative preferences. This principle aligns with rational norms upheld in all legal systems, where laws are presumed to be stable unless unequivocal evidence warrants their alteration

Several rational considerations support maintaining laws over time and across places.

Preserving legal continuity, which is seen as inherently rational from a legal perspective. Thus, maintaining existing laws often requires less justification than enacting new ones. For this reason, constitutional provisions established in previous generations are often upheld despite evolving circumstances

Ensuring historical continuity within society, fostering pride in the past and maintaining the virtues it represents. This continuity strengthens communal values and guards against societal shocks that might arise from sudden legal changes. While such shocks might only affect an intellectual minority, safeguarding the majority is prioritised.

Avoiding significant harm from altering laws compared to the potential issues with retaining them.

The Third Rule: Legislative rulings must not conflict—either in their initial issuance or continued application—with clear rational principles.

Scholars universally agree on this principle, though they differ on its theoretical basis. Some argue it stems from

Enforceable and Unenforceable Rulings

The Third Scenario: It is essential to distinguish between enforceable and unenforceable rulings. The establishment of a ruling within Islamic law does not necessarily entail its enforcement under all circumstances, according to certain jurisprudential perspectives. This parallels positive law, where some statutes are suspended—though not abolished—for a period due to emergencies or other factors.

To clarify: There are two perspectives in Islamic jurisprudence on this matter:

One of Them: Holds that every established ruling in Islamic law must inevitably be enforced and implemented by the governing authority. Failure to do so would amount to a nullification of the divine law.

Whilst the Other: Considers it permissible to suspend the enforcement of certain types of rulings—without nullifying them—due to valid factors justifying such suspension. During this period, an alternative ruling may be applied. Examples of such factors include: Leniency and accommodation for the people: This applies in cases where enforcement is

---

the intrinsic authority of reason, while others posit that divine law itself respects and incorporates these rational principles. Either way, it is evident that if a ruling conflicts with foundational rational norms, this conflict negates its validity according to Islamic law's principles.

not feasible, either intellectually—where implementation might lead to negative perceptions of the religion and its legislative principles—or practically—where enforcement might result in social disturbances or other detrimental consequences. Avoiding such outcomes is deemed more critical than enforcing the ruling itself. In such cases, the ruler is permitted to suspend the ruling, taking into consideration the overarching objectives of Islamic law.

And this approach finds evidence in religious texts and examples where leniency towards people is emphasised in line with their capacities and understanding. It is beyond the scope of this discussion to delve into all the instances that demonstrate this principle.

While this approach may not entirely address the question of the legitimacy of retaining a ruling—even without enforcing it—when it appears contrary to innate human nature (*fiṭra*), it does underscore the care that Islamic law takes to respect the general comprehension of the people. It affirms the commitment to ensuring that the principles of Islamic law are rooted in human nature and are never in conflict with it. This is presented as a fundamental and overarching approach to fostering an environment of virtue and wisdom in society while emphasising the pedagogical aspect of rulings and how they are received by the community.

Classification of Variable or Unenforceable Rulings

It is important to note that acknowledging the principle of categorising rulings as fixed or mutable, enforceable or unenforceable, does not grant every individual the liberty to determine which rulings fall into these categories. This task should be entrusted to a group of specialised jurists who are well-versed in the intellectual, historical, religious, and legal dimensions of rulings. Even if this method is occasionally prone to error, it serves to ensure reliability, protect the sanctity of the religion, and to safeguard the religious community from doubt, discord, and conflict. The purpose of discussing these classifications is merely to illustrate that within the framework of Islamic principles and values, there is scope for addressing ambiguous and unclear cases.

This concludes an overview of the legislative aspect of the religious worldview as derived from the fundamental religious texts and their fixed principles. Through this, the essence of religion—central to this section of the book—has been characterised.

It has become evident from the foregoing that religion, from its perspective, represents the consciousness of truth and its call. It came to unveil for humanity the grand truths of life, its purposes, and humanity's place within it.

It should be noted that this portrayal was not intended to encompass all dimensions of the religious worldview in its entirety. Instead, the aim of this chapter was to alert the seeker of truth to the broad outlines of the religious perspective, ensuring that they approach their personal stance—whether in affirmation or denial—with full clarity and understanding. Therefore, we have limited our discussion to what fulfills this objective.

All praise and gratitude is
due to Allah (the Mighty and Majestic),
and may He send his peace and blessings upon
Muḥammad and his pure progeny.

www.ingramcontent.com/pod-product-compliance
Lightning Source LLC
Chambersburg PA
CBHW060604080526
44585CB00013B/681